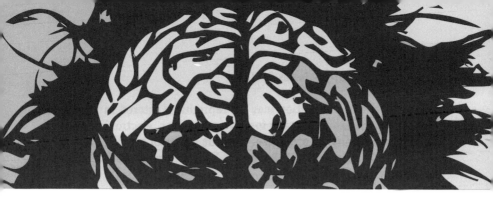

Mindblowers!

A Look Back at History
That Will Change the Way
You Look at the World Today

Chronicled by
Jim Rhine

TRIUMPH
BOOKS
CHICAGO

Contents

Part IV: Founding Fathers, Founding Follies

Part V: The Gilded Age

Part VI: A Century Turns

Part VII: Modern Times

Part VIII: Unusual Origins and Inventive Minds

Part IX: Say What? The Birth of Words and Phrases

Part X: Cool and Unusual People and Places

Part XI: Sports and Fatness

Part XII: Mindblowing Earth, Space, and Time

Part XIII: In Conclusion

Introduction

The purpose of this book is to bring to light some intriguing, almost forgotten moments of history and science that are unique, eye-opening, and always amazing. Some involve minor footnotes to our knowledge and others involve world-changing events, the hidden, unusual facts and contexts of which have been forgotten. Exploring these snippets of history, science, and other areas of knowledge will hopefully expand our appreciation of the past, the present, and the future.

None of these essays are to be considered definitive, complete, or even 100 percent accurate. As anyone who has studied the subject knows, history is inevitably shaped and unshaped by its chroniclers, regardless of how partisan or nonpartisan they attempt to be. Readers are directed to the bibliography at the end of the book for more complete information regarding the subjects herein. Listed there are excellent resources for following up on, and gaining more detailed treatments of, the characters, events, and issues touched on in these pages.

PART I
Early Times

Evolution: From the Big Bang to Modern Humans in 10 Easy Steps

The original Mindblower: how did it all begin and how did we get here?

Boom! Fifteen billion years ago it all begins as the cosmic explosion at the beginning of time called the Big Bang explodes the universe into existence in all directions. Zillions of galaxies, nebulas, suns, planets, moons, you, me, the 1968 Chrysler down the street—we're all there together at the start. All that has ever been or will ever be in our universe begins that day, hurtling out from this explosion toward the future.

By about 5 billion years ago, our Sun is burning hot within the Milky Way Galaxy and busily burping out its planets. One of these planets, Earth, is home to a miracle called *life*, as simple-celled organisms appear in an all-ocean world. This *life* is the beginning of us. These are our ancestors. Every living thing on Earth today is a direct descendant of these original ancient life-forms.

Slowly but inexorably, these simple early beings change and grow, change and grow, evolving into countless types of fish and other ocean life. We do so well that about 400 million years ago, we start dancing our way out of the ocean onto the sand. We're now semi-aquatic amphibians, with some of us as big as elephants, hanging around on the shore or in the water. Slowly we change into the reptiles, which don't have to go back into the water. We still need water to survive but we can stay on land. As reptiles, we give new meaning to the word *big* as we dominate the earth for the next 200 million years, changing and growing into innumerable varieties, including the amazing dinosaurs.

Suddenly, about 65 million years ago, just when we (dinosaur-reptiles) are having the time of our lives... *boom*! A second *boom*! Only this time it's a meteor and its massive impact and aftereffects wipe out countless creatures, including all the large dinosaurs, within a few years. Who's left? The fish, small amphibians, small reptiles, and little furry *us* reptiles, who are the forerunners of the mammals. Mammals survive where the dinosaurs do not. Other reptiles become birds. Insects have also appeared and also survive the massive second boom.

In the beginning, life was spawned by an explosion!

Over the next 60 million years, as little furry reptile-mammals, we change and grow and evolve into a cornucopia of the most amazing creatures ever: lions and tigers and bears and shrews and horses and camels and rats and cats and dogs and, most important for us, a special group of mammals, the apes. Now we're beginning to start to really look like ourselves. By about 5 million years ago, we apes have split into the gorillas, the chimpanzees, and other types of apes, including a small-bodied, big-brained ape living in southern Africa. Say "hi" to Grandpa because we are now the first real humanoids. It only took 14.99 billion years to get from the Big Bang to the Milky Way Galaxy to our Sun to planet Earth to simple ocean life to fish to amphibians to reptiles to mammals to apes to bigger-brained apes to the humanoids... us!

Now it's time to take this show on the road and see the world: to leave Africa and spread out over the whole Earth. And

we basically do it twice. The first time is about 1 million years ago, when we're known as the Neanderthals. This first wave of slow humanoid migration extends out of Africa into the Middle East, Europe, and a few parts beyond. But sadly, this migration is somehow not meant to last.

About 100,000 years ago, the second and most important humanoid migration out of Africa begins. This is the big one, the move that gives birth to all the humans who live throughout the entire globe today. And this migration is by the real and most complete *us* yet. The modern humans, also known as *Homo sapiens*. We're smaller than the Neanderthals who preceded us, but we're equipped with the newest and coolest evolutionary development so far, the power of speech. We follow in the footsteps of the Neanderthals and gradually replace them, and we travel farther than they ever did. The people of this *us* migration eventually travel to all the ends of the Earth, evolving into the many human ethnicities of the Earth today. The whole world is now truly ours.

Sometime around 15,000 to 10,000 years ago, another great and profound evolutionary change takes place for us: the discovery of agriculture. We can plant stuff and it'll grow, and we can eat it! This is a huge change for us as we no longer need to be nomadic or even semi-nomadic hunter-gatherers. We humans can begin to stay in one place for a while if we want to, planting crops, harvesting them, building communities, and multiplying our numbers. We still like to travel, but we can put down roots. The first villages and eventually cities form. Religion, technology, the arts, and other pursuits increase. Our brains, our bodies, and our knowledge grow as never before.

Finally, 6,000 years ago, history (which of course means written history) begins as we figure out an alphabet and how to write things down in order to record and remember all the many wondrous things we've been doing and seeing. We've arrived completely. Now we can write down our own story and begin to figure out the mindblowing mysteries that began with the Big Bang 15 billion years ago and that have brought us right on up to the present day. And that's where we begin.

The Biggest Killer in History

Who is it?

Was it Genghis Khan, whose forces may have killed 30 million in the 13th century? Hitler, who unleashed a madness that consumed 70 million lives? Stalin, with his systematic murder of 20 million souls?

None of these, if the Bible is to be believed and if we make a judgment based on percentages. It's Cain! Cain, the son of Adam and Eve, because according to Genesis chapter 4 in the Bible, he murdered one-fourth of the world's population at the time when he killed his brother Abel!

Not his brother's keeper: Cain wiped out one-quarter of the world's population when he killed his brother, Abel.

It Wasn't Just the Meteor, Boys

One often-mentioned hallmark at the end of the age of the dinosaurs and the rise of the mammals was a horrendous and catastrophic meteorite crash into Earth about 65 million years ago.

The theory goes that the dust cloud caused by the enormous explosion cooled the Earth to such an extent that the food supplies of the dinosaurs died and therefore so did the dinosaurs. But there's more to it than that.

> ... the cooler the eggs, the more males that were born.

Like many reptiles, the gender of baby dinosaurs depended on the temperature of the eggs in the nest after they were laid by the females. With warmer temperatures, more females were born. Conversely, the cooler the eggs, the more males that were born. With the cooler Earth caused by the meteorite dust cloud, the majority of the babies born were male. There were just not enough dinosaur chicks for all the dinosaur dudes! Too bad, guys.

But luckily for us, it was bye-bye, dinosaurs, hello, mammals!

During our time as humans over the last 4 million years, our average life expectancy was 19 years old! Indeed, for those millions of years, up until about 150,000 years ago, there were never more than 10,000 humans on the planet at any one time. We've increased just a little since then. But think about it. For 4 million years, the human race was made up of 10,000 19-year-olds!

"Which way to the teen club?"

The Original Bearded Lady

Ruling from about 1473–1458 BC, Ancient Egypt's first female Pharaoh and one of the first known ruling queens in history was Hatshepsut, the daughter of Thutmose I. With no word for a female ruler, she was actually crowned King Hatshepsut upon the death of her brother King Thutmose II, and she dressed in male regalia throughout her long reign, including wearing a false beard. Literally, Hatshepsut was the man!

> She dressed in male regalia throughout her long reign...

A successful Pharaoh and a prolific builder, she commissioned hundreds of building projects across Egyptian territory. Depictions of her in stone that remain clearly demonstrate her androgynous, masculine appearance and her ever-present beard.

You go, girl!

Old Man Ramses,
Can You Spare a Condom?

Egyptian Pharaoh Ramses II succeeded his grandfather Ramses I in 1290 BC and reigned for 66 years as one of the greatest Pharaohs in history until dying around the age of 90. He conducted the first known peace treaty in history (with the Hittites), was thought to be the Pharaoh during the time of the Biblical Exodus of the Hebrews, and has more remaining monuments to himself than any other Ancient

All's pharaoh in love and war: Ramses II reigned for 66 years before dying around the age of 90.

Egyptian ruler. In fact, he is styled by history as Ramses the Great.

He also had 200 wives, 96 sons, and 60 daughters, yet he outlived 13 different heirs he had designated to succeed him! Finally upon his death, he was succeeded by his son, Merneptah. This began a line of inept and weak kings who could not and did not maintain the pinnacle of imperial power to which Ramses II had raised Ancient Egypt.

Today, Ramses's mummy is in a Cairo mausoleum. It reveals an old, old man with a long face, a prominent nose, and a large jaw.

Humorously, a condom brand is today named for this Pharaoh who fathered over 150 children!

From the Jaws of Victory: Alexander and Darius

In 331 BC the Macedonian Greek military genius Alexander the Great with 40,000 troops faced off against the Persian Emperor Darius III with 250,000 men at the battle of Arbela (in modern day northern Iraq). Alexander had resurrected the glory of the ancient Greeks and had been kicking butt all over the Mediterranean, most of it at the expense of the Persians, and now he headed east toward the very heart of the Persian Empire itself. If Darius and the Persians could halt Alexander here, his threat to the world order would be over. If Alexander were to defeat Darius, he could conquer his way across the Persian Empire all the way to India. An important battle to say the least.

> If Darius and the Persians could halt Alexander here, his threat to the world order would be over.

On the day of the battle, the Greeks headed straight into the middle of the vast Persian forces, but just as suddenly as they engaged them, the Greeks made a hard right into the Persian left flank, attacking it fiercely. Darius countered by sending huge numbers of troops to try and encircle the Greek advance. But the Greeks answered this by raining down volley after murderous volley of arrows onto the Persians, decimating them. Oblivious to this, Darius sent more and more troops to try and surround the Greeks, leaving the middle part of his forces dangerously exposed.

Seeing the exposed Persian middle, Alexander himself led a daring cavalry charge directly at the Persian middle and directly at Darius himself! Under this sudden assault, Darius panicked and fled! His confused and leaderless army almost immediately followed him in retreat.

Alexander then chased Darius for 100 miles eastward, but before he could get his hands on him, one of Darius's own generals killed him for being a coward.

The mighty Persian Empire fell to Alexander virtually in a single day, and he and his victorious forces did indeed ultimately reach India, spreading a second wave of Greek culture across the world. But for all his conquering, Alexander himself didn't get to enjoy it for long, dying a few years later from a sudden fever at the age of 32.

If only the Persian Emperor Darius III had appreciated the power of archery!

One remnant of the vast areas conquered under Alexander is the Afghan city of Kandahar. Once the capital of Afghanistan, Kandahar is today the country's second largest city, and its name Kandahar is a local linguistic variation of the name of the man who conquered the region in 329 BC, Alexander the Great. That's leaving your mark 2,400 years later!

These Goods Are Hot!
Pompeii—AD 79

The destruction from the Italian volcano Vesuvius in AD 79 was devastating. Entire cities like Pompeii, Herculaneum, and Stabiae were destroyed. Thousands died, and the cities were covered in a vast, deep layer of volcanic ash.

Seventeen hundred years later, the site at Pompeii was awoken from its long slumber when it began to be uncovered with archeological endeavor.

> Dying to be rich: Victims of the volcano Vesuvius in AD 79 were miraculously preserved in volcanic ash.

Inside the remains of Pompeii was an extraordinary find: perfectly preserved humans, dead where they fell, their bodies miraculously preserved by the sheer heat, volcanic fury, and dust. There, caught in their final moments and perfectly preserved in the volcanic ash, were the last survivors of the doomed cities. None more obviously and tragically hilarious than the bodies identified as looters, frozen with their intended loot still in their grasp where they fell!

Literally, caught in the act for all time.

PART II
Stuck in the
Middle Ages with You

On the Wings of Angels

It wasn't until around AD 350 that angels were given wings. Until that time, all the depictions of angels in art were indistinguishable from humans. Finally someone got the great idea to copy pagan images of winged creatures in order to make angels special and capable of all their flying around and visiting everybody and the like. Christian angels of modern times are flying around on ancient pagan wings!

Basil the Bulgar-Slayer and the Kingdom of the Blind

By the beginning of the 11th century AD, the Bulgars (the ethnic group that today occupies Bulgaria) had become a national military and cultural force to be reckoned with in southeastern Europe. Most of the land of their emerging and growing empire had been taken from the Byzantines over the last few hundred years, and Byzantine Emperor Basil II was determined to reverse this trend.

Over the next dozen years, the Byzantines and the Bulgars battled, but with neither gaining the upper hand. Finally, at the battle of Kleidion (today near the border of southern Bulgaria and northern Greece) in 1014, the Byzantines defeated the Bulgar army and captured 20,000 men. What followed was what would forever give Basil his nickname for the ages.

An eye for an eye? Basil the Bulgar-Slayer made sure he proved his point at the Battle of Kleidion.

Basil had the captured men blinded one after another, leaving every 100th man one eye to see in order to guide the others home!

Needless to say, on the way home countless thousands died of accident, starvation, or worse until only a paltry fraction of the original force arrived back safely. When the Bulgar king Samuil saw the tiny remnant of his once mighty army staggering home blinded and completely defeated, he collapsed and died of a heart attack!

The Bulgars didn't bother anyone again for a very, very long time.

Basil the Bulgar-Slayer

Infested with Religious Fervor: The Death of Thomas à Becket

In 1170, the Archbishop of Canterbury, Thomas à Becket, was murdered by a group of knights who thought they were doing the bidding of their king, Henry II. You see, Henry and Thomas had actually been great friends for a long time until one day when Henry made Thomas the archbishop. From that time on, Thomas seems to have gotten religion and was often at odds with the wishes of the king. After one particularly exasperating moment when Thomas opposed the wishes of the king to limit the power of the church, Henry angrily pondered aloud, "Will no one rid me of this meddlesome priest?"

Hoping to curry favor with the king, a group of Henry's knights then tracked Thomas to Canterbury Cathedral. There inside the church, they attacked him and struck him down with their swords, gruesomely killing him at the very altar itself. Upon hearing of the murder, King Henry feigned shock at the killing and actually eventually went through an elaborate sackcloth and ashes routine to assuage his guilty conscience. The knights who thought they were doing the king a favor were disgraced and ostracized. Eventually a few miracles were accorded old Thomas, and his crypt in Canterbury Cathedral became a pilgrimage site. In fact, that's where everybody is headed in Chaucer's *The Canterbury Tales* (1340), on a pilgrimage to Thomas's crypt when they all tell their tales.

But that's not the whole story. Thomas and Henry had been great friends, but after Thomas was appointed Archbishop of Canterbury, he really did start to take the religion stuff seriously. For one thing, he no longer bathed, wanting to be as natural as God made him.

> ... he no longer bathed, wanting to be as natural as God made him.

Indeed, when the monks of the cathedral prepared his body for burial after his murder, they were stunned to find under his fabulous robes that Thomas was wearing a hair shirt, and beneath that, filthy, never-washed underwear bursting with thousands upon thousands of lice!

To promote religious humility, Thomas had intentionally fostered the growth of the lice amidst his personal filth so that the constant pain of the zillions of lice feeding on him would prevent him from feeling any personal pride!

Talk about being infested with religious fervor.

Too Much of a Lion

King Richard I (the Lion-Hearted) (1157–1199), the English Norman king, is famous mostly for his military campaigns in France and his leadership of the Third Crusade. Styled the "Lion-Hearted," he is the epitome of medieval knighthood and bravery and considered almost universally a heroic warrior with few equals. His greatest success and his greatest failure was the Third Crusade. Leading this campaign, Richard's forces took Sicily, Cyprus, and wide swaths of Palestine before being halted only a few miles from Jerusalem.

Usually the cause for this defeat is blamed on the quitting of the French King Philip II and the Austrian Duke Leopold V and their troops from the battlefield before the assault on Jerusalem, leaving Richard with a much smaller force. But while these actions were definitely a factor, the defeat had a more serious and sinister cause.

When Richard and his forces took the fortress of Acre in Northern Palestine in 1192 as their first mainland conquest, they captured close to 3,000 Muslim soldiers. Unable to feed or imprison these prisoners for long, and knowing full well that if released they would fight his forces again, Richard ordered their execution—but not just any execution. Despite standing

> Crusader rabid: Richard the Lion-Hearted's talent for war and glory may very well have lost him his most precious prize of all.

prisoner-exchange agreements with the Muslims, Richard had the prisoners paraded out to a clearing within view of the remaining Muslim forces, and a bloody spectacle was unleashed. Three thousand Muslim soldiers (and hundreds more of their wives and children) were executed in a single ruthless act.

As word spread through the Muslim world of this bloodbath, it transformed the hereto divided Muslims in a critical way. Richard's barbaric, despicable act convinced them that there could be no mercy, no prisoners, and no prisoner exchanges. All Christians, soldiers and civilians alike, would forever face no quarter and no mercy. The Muslims swore bloody revenge and unity against the dishonorable infidel Crusaders.

Some historians believe that without this barbaric act, it would have been much easier for the Crusaders to defeat the

RICHARD. I.

fractious Muslims and take Jerusalem, the ultimate prize. Instead, the angry and energized Muslim forces settled their own squabbles and aligned under Saladin to hammer the Crusaders. Additionally, other arguments over who got the glory and the spoils of war caused a rift that indeed resulted in Philip and Leopold pulling out of the Crusade and heading home with their troops.

Richard and his own troops continued valiantly on, but despite some impressive victories on the way, it became obvious that in no way did Richard have enough men to take Jerusalem, let alone hold it if he did.

Defeated, Richard stopped 10 miles from Jerusalem and refused to even look upon the city from a high vantage point, stating that God had determined that he was not to be the one to liberate the city, so therefore he would not gaze upon it.

Eventually Richard signed a peace treaty with Saladin that allowed unarmed Christian pilgrims access to the Holy City. Every unarmed Christian pilgrim, that is, except Richard himself. He alone was barred by Saladin's order. When Richard finally left Palestine to head home, the Third Crusade was over. On the way home, Richard was captured by his former ally, the Austrian Duke Leopold, and held for ransom for two years. Finally released, he spent little time in his kingdom of England, instead fighting for the last five years of his life to regain territory lost in France during his years away. He died in 1199 at the age of 41 from an arrow wound received fighting near the northern French town of Chalus. He's even buried in France. It's estimated that Richard probably spent less than six months in England during his entire ten-year reign as its king.

Perhaps he should have been a little less barbaric and a little more Britannic.

As Long As We're Here:
The Inglorious Fourth Crusade

On their way to Jerusalem to wrest it from the control of the Muslims in 1202, the so-called Christian Knights of the Fourth Crusade stopped off in Byzantium (modern day Istanbul, Turkey), then the richest city in the Christian world. They were about to develop a serious case of Crusadus Interruptus.

With no way to pay the Venetians who had transported them there, they went along with the Venetians' idea to sack

> Christian Knights looted and pillaged the largest and richest city in the Christian world.

Byzantium to pay for their costs! Incredibly, so-called Christian Knights on their way to free the Holy Land from the Muslims severely looted and pillaged the largest and richest city in the Christian world.

In fact, they never moved on to Muslim territory. They divided up the Byzantine Empire into a few mini-kingdoms and ruled for a few decades before the Byzantines eventually overthrew them and regained power.

So much for the Fourth "Crusade."

The Children's Crusade

Of the many medieval military expeditions termed Crusades, in which Christian Knights and others tried to wrest control of the Holy Land from the Muslims and then hang on to it, none is perhaps more tragic and ironic than the Children's Crusade of 1212.

Numerically, the Children's Crusade ranked as the fifth of these efforts but differed from the first four in a crucial way. Whereas the first four had been military campaigns, the Children's Crusade began when two young boys, one in France (Stephen) and one in Germany (Nicholas), simultaneously and independently had visions of Jesus telling them to lead Crusades to wrest Jerusalem from the Muslims, but this time it would be done with love, not by force of arms.

As a result of his preaching in France and the supposed performing of miracles, Stephen attracted a following of up to 30,000 children and other hangers-on who followed him southward to the French port of Marseille. There it had been predicted that the sea would part for them and the children would march in triumph directly to Jerusalem itself.

When the sea did not part, several sailing merchants offered to transport the children for free, and so Stephen and as many of his followers as could be stuffed onto the boats departed from Marseille. Sadly, rather than transport the children to Palestine in the East, the merchants sailed directly south across the Mediterranean Sea to Muslim Tunisia in North Africa and promptly sold Stephen and all his followers into slavery!

Meanwhile, Nicholas, the young German boy, had preached and performed miracles of his own and had gathered a following of about 40,000. Independent of the French children, Nicholas led his group from Germany, ostensibly with a plan to cross the Alps, enter Italy, march down to the bottom of the country, and again wait for the grace of God to transport them across the Mediterranean Sea to the Holy Land.

Sadly, while crossing the Alps, thousands of Nicholas's followers died from exposure and hunger. The few thousand remaining that made it into Italy half-mad with starvation were feared by the local populations, who attacked them and drove them off and away from their cities. A paltry few hundred finally made it to Italy's southern coast where some few were freed from their Crusader oaths by the Pope, but where most of them suffered the same cruel fate as Stephen and his group in France, being tricked and sold into slavery and never setting foot in the Holy Land.

> One cultural offshoot of this tragedy is the legend of the Pied Piper of Hamelin, which has its roots indirectly in the Children's Crusade.

One cultural offshoot of this tragedy is the legend of the Pied Piper of Hamelin, which has its roots indirectly in the Children's Crusade. Perhaps as a weird way to subconsciously cope with the fact that they allowed so many of their children to blindly march off to their deaths or worse, the legend of the Pied Piper appeared in Europe shortly after the Children's Crusade.

The legend, of course, tells the story of the pipe-playing man who comes to the town of Hamelin in Germany to rid it of its many rats. After the Piper did his job and rid the town of its rats by leading them all away with his pipe playing, the town's elders foolishly refused to pay him as promised. To take his revenge, the Pied Piper returned the next day and again began playing his pipe, only this time he led all of the town's children away; and just like the disastrous undertakings of young Stephen and Nicholas and their followers in the Children's Crusade, they are never seen or heard from ever again!

Killing about one-third the population of Europe (about 25 million people) in the 1300s, the Black Death was a form of bubonic plague that probably came west with Mongol invaders and eventually arrived in Europe in the mid-1300s. The plague itself was caused by a bacterium that lived inside fleas that lived on sewer rats, and, unfortunately for us, the fleas can also live on humans.

Whole cities, towns, and villages were decimated by the disease, which could strike a perfectly healthy individual in the morning, and after about 12 excruciating hours in which the bacterium coursed through the body of the doomed, amid massive internal bleeding and blackening of the skin (hence the name the Black Death), the poor soul would die.

Of course, the utter lack of hygiene and garbage control, the tightly cramped living spaces of the cities and towns, and generally miserable medieval conditions all contributed greatly to the spread of the deadly disease.

But there is one overlooked factor. No cats. Because most Europeans were illiterate, superstitious louts, many people saw cats as the companions of the Devil or as familiars to witches. Therefore, for centuries cats were killed when-

> Kill the cat; kill the village. Entire cities, towns, and villages were lost to the ravages of the Black Death in the 1300s.

ever or wherever they were found, in much the same way that people today might kill a cockroach. Sadly for the citizens of

Europe, because of their irrational fear of cats, the local rodent populations raged unchecked. As the Black Plague–infected rats and fleas made their way into Europe from Asia, their terrible bacterial companion found ready rodent populations to spread the disease.

So when you're petting your little kitty cat, remember that if the citizens of medieval Europe had only appreciated our furry little feline friends a bit more, we might never have heard of the term the *Black Death*.

This Is a Trippy Village

During the Middle Ages, around 1300, a strange phenomenon occurred after humans often unknowingly ate bread infested with ergot fungus. Unbeknownst to these bread eaters, ergot fungus is similar in chemical structure to other hallucinogens of the fungus and mushroom family. As a result, after eating the infested bread, whole villages would begin tripping out, wildly shrieking and seeing demons and devils.

The phenomenon was so severe it gained the name St. Anthony's Fire, in which priests would come in and try to calm the village and exorcise the demons. Some scholars even suggest that the affected young girls behind the Salem Witch Trials may have been the victims of ergot poisoning, which led to their visions and hallucinations.

The ergot fungus grows on rye and other grains during times of dampness and humidity and was just cooked unknowingly right into the bread without losing any of its hallucinogenic potency. Sadly, long-term exposure and poisoning by ergot fungus causes convulsions and gangrene, resulting in death. In modern times, scientific awareness of the causes, and careful control of grains in damp or humid conditions, has all but wiped out the outbreaks.

But can you imagine riding into a small village or town during the Middle Ages and having everyone in the town, men, women, and children alike, tripping out of their minds on hallucinogens? It's almost enough to make you start a low-carb, bread-free diet!

Thanks for Changing the World, Now Pay Up!

Johannes Gutenberg, the 15th-century German inventor and metal worker, is best known for his contributions to the art and science of printing by developing a system of moveable type (basically block letters). He also pioneered a metal alloy with which to pour and mold the type, and a new kind of printing press modeled on one used in winemaking. With these advances, Gutenberg transformed the world and history by creating a means for rapid printing of written materials, setting off an information explosion that fed the growing Renaissance and the end of the Middle Ages.

While printers in both China and Korea had been using a form of moveable type for years before Gutenberg, the intricacies of their languages slowed their efforts to make full use of it. Gutenberg on the other hand was able to use his new invention to launch an explosion of printed works capped most magnificently around 1455 by the now famous Gutenberg Bibles, the first mass-produced works in history. Today these Bibles are generally regarded as the most valuable books in the world, and only about 60 are believed to be left in existence.

With Gutenberg's invention, books, other printed works, and ideas themselves traveled across Europe and the world at a speed never seen before. The spread of this knowledge nurtured the growing Renaissance and laid the foundation for the Scientific Revolution as well. As Gutenberg's books spread, so did the liberating power of literacy and knowledge. He truly changed the world as never before. There was only one problem with old Gutenberg's plan.

While he was an ingenious and clever man, Gutenberg was not a wealthy one. In order to get most of his plans and schemes going, he had to borrow large sums of money from those who thus became his "partners." One of these partners, Johann Fust, was impatient that he wasn't making money more quickly off his substantial investment in Gutenberg and his inventions. Taking him to court, Fust ended up winning the lawsuit and forced Gutenberg to pay up or else, with interest.

With Gutenberg unable to pay off his debt, Fust took possession of most of his equipment and business ventures. Fust then continued to print books and materials using Gutenberg's equipment, and the first book printed in Europe with the name of the printer on it bore the name of Johann Fust, not Gutenberg.

> ... the first book printed in Europe with the name of the printer on it bore the name of Johann Fust...not Gutenberg.

With his inventions, Gutenberg changed the very course of history but never made a dime himself as a result! Johannes Gutenberg died in 1468, hardly a decade after the invention of his world-changing machine. Maybe before he died he should have written (and published) a tell-all, best-selling book about his own life!

C'mon, Martin! How Long You Gonna Be in There?

Martin Luther was without a doubt one of the most influential humans in history. A German priest, theologian, and religious reformer, his most influential written work was the "95 Theses" against Papal indulgences and other less-than-spiritual activities of the Catholic Church. The publication of the "95 Theses" launched the Protestant Reformation in 1517 and set in motion a whole host of other social, economic, and political changes that are still being played out to this day.

What many people do not know about Martin Luther is that he was often constipated, a fact he alluded to himself in his writings, and spent much of his time "in contemplation" sitting on the john! Recently, archeologists working on the remains of Martin Luther's house in Wittenberg, Germany, have discovered the toilet where it is believed he wrote the "95 Theses" and other important works.

> Flushed with success: Luther's "95 Theses," most of which were conceptualized on the john, launched the Protestant Reformation in 1517.

At this point, visitors to Luther's home will not be allowed to sit on the toilet, but one wonders if one day old Martin had not been a bit short of toilet paper, would there have been "96 Theses"?

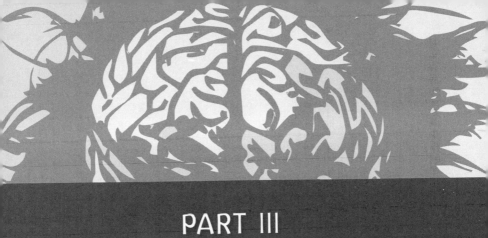

PART III
New World,
New Mindblowers

African Americans: Who Was First?

Who was the first African to set foot in the Americas? There are legends of African explorers coming to America from West Africa long before Columbus, but none of these can as yet be confirmed, as there is no archeological evidence to support the legends.

Perhaps the best case can be made for a black man named Pedro Alonzo Nino, a Spaniard of African descent who was the pilot of the Santa Maria, one of the three ships that crossed the Atlantic Ocean during Christopher Columbus's first voyage. As Columbus's navigator, he would have arrived here in the Americas in October 1492, thus making him the first known African to make the trip. Indeed, numerous free African sailors and soldiers accompanied the first waves of Spanish conquest of the Americas. It was decades later, after native populations had died off, that Africans were brought to the Caribbean islands and the American mainland as slaves. Could Pedro and these other black Conquistadors have been the first Africans in the Americas?

> ... we're all Africans.

Ironically, the truth is much simpler than that. And that truth is, we're all Africans. We all originally come from Africa. It's a proven genetic fact. So in that regard, the first "Africans" in the Americas would be the direct ancestors of the Native American Indians who crossed the Bering Ice Bridge from Asia into what's now Alaska around 50,000 BC!

400 Spaniards vs. 25 Million Aztecs

Around 1520, Hernando Cortez and a few hundred men came ashore in what is now Mexico and conquered an Aztec empire of 25 million people. How the heck did they do that?

When Cortez came ashore he quickly defeated a group of Native Americans who had a long history of antagonism toward the Aztecs. After defeating them, he made them an offer they couldn't refuse: either join him against the Aztecs or die where they stood. They joined. He also found a woman who hated the Aztecs for selling her into slavery and was willing to work as his translator. Finally, and perhaps most importantly, he learned of an old Aztec legend about the prophesied return of an ancient god from across the sea. Hmmmmm. Taking advantage of all three of these conditions—native allies, a reliable translator, and his ability to pretend to be the returning god that had been foretold—Cortez was welcomed by Emperor Montezuma into the Aztec capital, Tenochtitlan (modern day Mexico City). It was a fabulous island in the middle of a lake, joined

to the mainland by many causeway bridges, and was larger and wealthier than anything the Spaniards had ever seen. Taking advantage of the confused Aztecs, Cortez almost immediately took Montezuma prisoner and threateningly demanded a fabulous ransom in gold for his release, which was given. Sadly

Germ warfare—conquistador style: Hernando Cortez and his vastly outnumbered Spanish troops toppled an Aztec empire of millions.

for the Aztecs, though, giving the Spaniards gold was like pouring gasoline on a fire in an effort to put it out.

Before he could take full advantage of this new fabulous opportunity for plunder and conquest, Cortez and some of his men had to return to the coast to face Spanish soldiers sent to arrest him for going beyond his mandate. His superiors sent him to investigate, not to conquer or advance on the capital city.

Facing these troops, Cortez's forces defeated them and he gave them the same choice he gave the conquered natives: join him in his war of conquest or die on the spot. Being the conquistadors that they were, the survivors swore allegiance to Cortez and his cause.

Meanwhile, the Spaniards left behind in the Aztec capital had massacred many Aztecs, and the Aztecs were no longer amused or convinced of the divinity of the Spaniards. Cortez returned to the capital to find the Spaniards besieged by the Aztecs. Fighting his way to the Spaniards' position, he tried to have his prisoner, Montezuma, talk to the attacking Aztecs, but they would have none of it. They rained rocks down on them all, killing Montezuma.

That night the Spaniards decided to make a run for it. They'd grab as much gold as they could and race to the beach. Unfortunately, as they made a run for it, the Aztecs attacked! Hundreds of Spaniards died trying to cross the causeway bridges and flee. Many of the Spanish soldiers drowned when knocked off the bridges into the lake, weighed down by all their precious gold!

At the coast only a few hundred Spaniards remained, and a very angry Aztec empire was coming after them. Many of the Spanish wanted to just take what they had and leave, but

Cortez rallied his soldiers for a counter-attack, building flat-boats with which to attack the Aztec capital island.

And then a miracle happened. A miracle for the Spaniards, but an absolute catastrophe for the Aztecs. One of the Spaniards killed in the attempt to flee had smallpox, and in only a matter of days the virus had spread like wildfire through the Aztec population. Having been out of the genetic mainstream of the Old World for 50,000 years, the Aztecs fell prey to the virus with a gruesome vengeance. As Cortez and his remaining men and their Native American allies counter-attacked the Aztec capital, the defending Aztec soldiers could barely stand due to this new plague! Seizing this unholy advantage, Cortez and his men attacked the Aztecs with renewed fury, slaughtering hundreds of thousands of them as they smashed, pillaged, and destroyed the capital city and conquered the Aztecs.

And that's how Cortez and only a few hundred men conquered an empire of 25 million. They had a little help from Old World microbes.

In a strangely ironic quid pro quo, the Native Americans did give syphilis to the Europeans who took it home, where it killed and maimed millions.

You Can't Take It with You, Francisco

Francisco Pizarro, the Spanish Conquistador, is famous as the man who conquered the Incas in Peru in the 1530s. Similar to what Cortez had done in Mexico, Pizarro managed to capture the Inca emperor, Atahualpa, and hold him as a captive, thus being able to use him as a bargaining tool against the native Incas while he conquered and plundered the kingdom. Despite the fact that Atahualpa arranged to have an enormous ransom in gold and silver paid to Pizarro and his men, Pizarro unnecessarily had the Inca emperor brutally strangled to death after holding him prisoner for close to a year.

> Dishonor among thieves: Francisco Pizarro conquered the Incas in Peru, but he didn't live long enough to savor his victory.

As Pizarro and his men plundered the Inca empire and shipped some of the treasure back to Spain, a fierce argument erupted between Pizarro and some of his fellow Conquistadors over how to divvy up the loot and the land. During the ensuing conflict, Pizarro had the leader of the rebels, his former right-hand man, executed. Naturally, with men of such charming dispositions, shortly thereafter friends of the executed man broke in on Pizarro having dinner and stabbed him to death!

This man, who had changed world history by conquering a kingdom of millions and who had ruthlessly betrayed the Inca emperor after he had given the Spanish everything they had asked for and more, was killed by his own men, never living to enjoy the benefits of his stolen treasure!

I Say, Ol' Chap, Can I Borrow a Boat?

In Central America there is only one country with English as an official language, the nation of Belize. The reason for this is that despite the heavy presence of Spanish conquest throughout the region over the years, Belize itself was first "settled" by a group of shipwrecked English pirates in 1638.

Despite sporadic tension and attacks from Native Americans and the Spanish, this de facto English outpost survived and eventually grew into the crown colony of British Honduras. Begun as the byproduct of a buccaneer shipwreck, it was the last British colonial territory on the American mainland until it became an independent country in 1981.

From pirate pit stop to crown colony.

She's in Charge of Sales Here in Africa

In West Africa in the 1700s, the slave trade was thriving. White and black greed had propelled slavery to new heights in this part of the world.

Whereas in the past, slavery had been a part of African life, i.e., defeated enemies were made slaves (as in many cultures, including the Ancient Greeks and Romans), things had reached the point where African nations would go to war solely to defeat the enemy and sell them to whitey for cash and goods. As the lands of the New World called for more and more slaves, this had become big business.

Most of these facts are probably at least partly known or even well known by most and are sadly not surprising. But the fact that at one time one of the main middlemen doing the wheeling and dealing was a woman may not be so well known. That's right; a woman was one of the rich millionaire slave merchants on the African side. An African woman named Fenda Lawrence was in charge of sales.

The West African areas at the center of the slave trade in the 1700s were some of the few places in the world where matriarchy (social and political rule by women) was still in place instead of the more familiar patriarchy (rule by men). Women were often the monarchs, the judges, the priests, and the merchants. And they were also polygamous. Rich West African women often had multiple husbands.

And at the top of the booming slave trade in Gambia, Fenda was cashing in on it and making enormous profits.

Not only was Fenda an unlikely successful slave merchant

A shame on both our houses: Due to white and black greed, the slave trade thrived in West Africa in the 1700s.

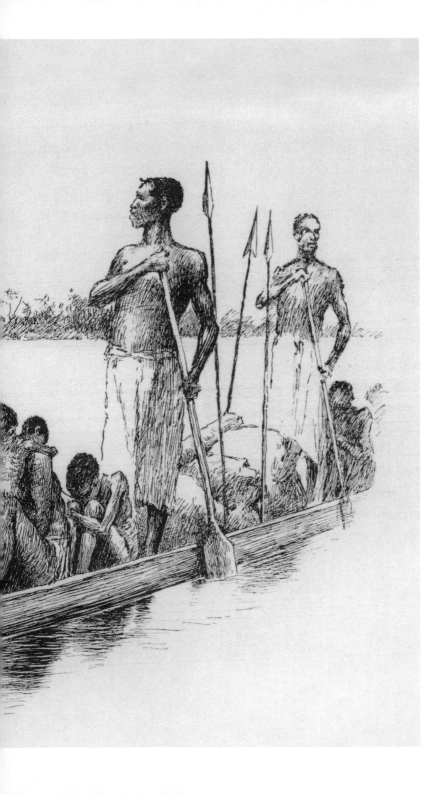

from our modern point of view, she actually did something quite extraordinary around 1772. She took a voyage to the American South, presumably as a privileged guest of plantation owners, to check out the American side of the business. Incredibly, during a time of horrible slavery, this West African black woman may have toured the southern American colonies in style to be fêted with gala banquets and receptions, and generally treated to all the honors and favors of a cherished friend and economic ally. Here was one black woman who could ride through the South without being touched because she was one of the people selling blacks into slavery!

After all the "fun," it can only be assumed she returned to Africa and resumed her slave-trade empire. One note, though: while in America, she did reportedly have to carry a certificate with her at all times, just in case she got stopped. The certificate, a piece of paper, explained that she was not a slave, but an African trader and slave seller from across the sea. I'm so glad they had that all straightened out.

Less than 150 years later it would all be over, and the African slave trade and Fenda Lawrence would thankfully vanish into history.

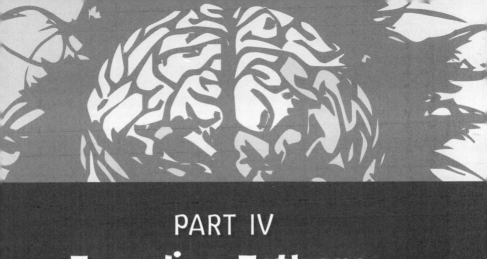

PART IV
Founding Fathers, Founding Follies

The *Mayflower*'s Out of Beer! We Gotta Stop!

In 1620, when the religious refugees known as the Pilgrims set out from England for the Americas, they had two possible destinations: one in Virginia and a secondary emergency location to the north. According to records written onboard the ship, a shortage of beer caused the leaders of the ship to forego Virginia, and the *Mayflower* then landed at the secondary emergency site in the Plymouth, Massachusetts, area instead. Now why would a boatload of non-drinking religious types be drinking beer anyway? And why would running short of it precipitate the need to stop at a secondary location, away from their primary destination?

Plymouth Rock: America's first beer run.

In 1620 it could take you up to two months to cross the Atlantic Ocean from England to the Americas, and at the time water quality was notoriously bad. The only reliable liquid available was barreled beer, and it was loaded into the *Mayflower* in quantity. Bad weather plagued the *Mayflower*, and after a couple of months at sea with a bunch of drunken Puritans, you'd come ashore just about anywhere, too! Obviously while foundering about at sea, they ran out of drinkable liquids—their beer—and had to come ashore to find water, thus leading to the founding of Plymouth Colony in Massachusetts instead of Virginia.

Old habits die hard, though. Even after finding a ready supply of fresh water after coming ashore in Massachusetts, one of the very first things the Pilgrims did was build a brewery!

Old Muttonhead:
Fun Facts about George Washington

Most of the main facts about our first president are well known and readily discoverable in the nearest encyclopedia. But what are some of the lesser known (and perhaps more intriguing) facts about the "Father of Our Country"? Here are a few that don't often get mentioned in the typical short biography.

He was a man of prayer and great courage.

He was one of the few founding fathers who freed his slaves.

He grew marijuana.

He liked to go fishing.

He liked to drink beer, and in an effort to bolster confidence in American

George Washington: the hard-charging, hard-praying, pot-using, beer-swilling, gambling Father of His Country.

products, he told LaFayette in a letter that he would "henceforth, only drink American porter beer."

He loved to gamble. A lifelong diary-writer, he also kept detailed personal account books, which included his card winnings and losses. One day in 1772, he noted, for example, that he had won $7.50 "at cards" and a few days later again noted "cash won at cards at Mrs. Calvert's." Additionally, he often bet on horse races and was active in the various state and regional lotteries of his time, which financed construction of schools, public buildings, and even churches.

He loved to dance and host parties, big and small.

He was a Freemason. Thirty-three of the generals who served under him during the Revolutionary War were Freemasons, as were his foreign allies Lafayette and von Steuben. He was sworn in as President wearing his Masonic apron, and when he died, Washington was buried in a Masonic funeral.

He's credited with introducing the mule to America.

He was an avid collector and player of marbles (called "small bowls" at the time), as were John Adams and Thomas Jefferson.

He owned dogs named Sweet Lips, Drunkard, and Tipsy.

Land rich but cash poor, he had to borrow money to travel to his first inauguration in New York City.

At his second inauguration, he gave the shortest inaugural address ever delivered by a president, only 135 words. Some speculate that this was a result of his lifelong problem with bad teeth, of which he had perhaps only one real one at the time of this inauguration. Contrary to popular belief, his teeth weren't made of wood (although part of them may have been), but more likely they were made from rhinoceros and hippopotamus ivory, as well as whalebone and deer antlers.

His vice president, John Adams, regularly called him Old Muttonhead.

All in all, he was a remarkable man. He was the commander in chief of the Continental Army during the American Revolution, served as the chairman of the Constitutional Convention that established the American system of government, and voluntarily relinquished power after serving two terms as president, thereby establishing an important precedent. He may have been Old Muttonhead, but he truly was the Father of His Country.

Give Me Liberty or Give Me Death! Unless You're My Wife

Patrick Henry of Virginia was one of the most prominent and radical politicians of the American Revolutionary period and is famous for some of the most stirring and rousing quotes and speeches from that time. His early agitations were always in pursuit of more liberty and rights for the colonies, and always at the expense of the king and Great Britain, as exemplified by such great quotes as "I'm not a Virginian, I'm an American" and "If this be treason, make the most of it!"

But perhaps his greatest quote, and one historians credit with rallying the Virginians to the American Revolutionary cause, came in March 1775 when he gave a speech before the sharply divided House of Burgesses, the colonial government of Virginia at the time. After a rousing rebuttal of those who wanted to adopt a path of appeasement, Patrick Henry ended his brilliant speech in favor of revolution against crown and king with the immortal words, "Is life so dear or peace so sweet as to be purchased at the price of chains and slavery? Forbid it, Almighty God! I know not what course others may take, but as for me, give me liberty or give me death!"

Wow! What a guy! What a rallying cry! The crowd jumped up and cheered, "To arms! To arms!" and Virginians were now fully committed to the Revolution that would end in the birth of the United States of America. Patrick Henry himself would go on to be the first governor of Virginia, a leading proponent of the Constitution's Bill of Rights, and eventually died at the age of 63 in 1799. But was that all there was to the story of this freedom-loving guy? Unfortunately not!

This "Give me liberty or give me death" guy actually kept his own wife locked up in the basement of their house for the last four years of her life!

Sadly, after giving birth to several children, Patrick Henry's wife, Sarah, began to lose her mind and abuse her young children, by neglect and even sometimes by physical violence. As his wife got worse and worse, and it was obvious that she was a threat to herself and her children, Patrick Henry had to make a terrible decision.

> There in that cellar, Sarah Henry lived out the last four years of her life...

The facilities for the mentally ill in the 18th century were notoriously little more than nuthouse prisons where the insane and enfeebled were treated like animals. Unwilling to face the prospect of placing his wife in such a place, Patrick Henry decided that if his wife was to be locked up for her own good, it would be in the family cellar with all the comforts that could be maintained for her there. But still locked up, away from the children and others.

There in that cellar, Sarah Henry lived out the last four years of her life until her death at age 35, often screaming and wailing to be let out into the light of day.

One wonders if Patrick Henry may have heard the line "Give me liberty or give me death!" once or twice himself before he delivered it to the Virginia House of Burgesses and history!

Like Son, Like Father, Like Dead

When Alexander Hamilton, the guy on the U.S. ten-dollar bill, was shot and killed in a duel in 1804, he was shot on the exact same spot where his son had died in a duel three years before. His son had died there on the same dueling field of Weehawken, New Jersey, defending his father's honor.

Hamilton himself had been born out of wedlock in the West Indies and had served as Washington's chief of staff during the Revolution. Eventually he became one of the most influential Americans in the setting up of the Constitution and the American banking system, serving as the U.S. government's first Secretary of the Treasury under new President George Washington. He was also involved in the first political sex scandal in American history (he was blackmailed after having an affair with a married woman), and he was mortally wounded in his famous duel by none other than the vice president of the U.S. at the time, Aaron Burr!

It's a long story; mostly it had to do with Hamilton bad-mouthing Burr in favor of other candidates on numerous occasions, over many years, and finally making scurrilous comments about Burr and his own daughter. Finally Burr had enough and called Hamilton out to that open New Jersey field at dawn. There Burr shot him, and Hamilton died a short time later. Burr himself did not go unscathed by the event. Dueling was illegal in most states, and Burr eventually found his political career destroyed and himself a fugitive from justice. He would go on to be involved in a treasonous plot to take over the western U.S and had to leave the country for many years to avoid the scorn (and possible criminal prosecution) of his fellow Americans. Get yourself a good biography of Hamilton and Burr, and prepare yourself for two of the greatest, yet tragic, personal journeys in American history.

Interestingly, a few years before the famous Hamilton/Burr duel, Alexander Hamilton got into a ferocious argument with future President James Monroe. The anger between them reached such a fever pitch that a duel seemed almost inevitable. That is until one man stepped in and calmed the waters between them and helped them make peace. Who was this great peacemaker who stepped between Hamilton and Monroe and prevented them from meeting on the dueling field of honor? His name was Aaron Burr!

The field of "honor" claims more lives. Aaron Burr shot Alexander Hamilton in their infamous duel in 1804, but Burr lived out his life a virtual fugitive.

Boiling Mad

The American Revolutionary War general known as "Mad Anthony" Wayne earned his nickname from his many bold leadership decisions during the Revolution. A surveyor, like George Washington was before the war, he quickly became involved by organizing a company of soldiers to help fight for the independence of the colonies.

During the conflict, at numerous battle sites like Fort Ticonderoga, Stony Point, West Point, and others, he more than earned his "Mad" sobriquet with daring (some would say foolhardy) raids and military operations against the British that more than often turned the tide in the Colonial army's favor. Naturally, of course, this made him a hero to his men and to the general population of colonists as well.

After the war he continued his winning ways against British forces and their Native American allies who had refused to leave the Northwest Territory as agreed to in the peace agreements that had ended the Revolutionary War. Following these successes, he also spent time in politics, but perhaps the most interesting part of his story for our purposes came after his death from gout in 1796 and his burial in Erie, Pennsylvania.

Thirteen years later in 1809, "Mad Anthony" Wayne's son Isaac traveled to Erie to disinter his father's remains and transport them to the family crypt in Radnor, Pennsylvania, some miles distant. Upon his arrival, the people of Erie were extremely reluctant to give up the body of such an important war hero. After all, his remains had been there for more than a dozen years, why disturb them now? Finally, though, the townspeople could not argue with the request of the dead general's son.

But then a very strange turn of events occurred. Upon disinterring his father's body, Isaac discovered that his father's corpse was both very well preserved and also very long and stiff. Indeed, the small coffin that Isaac had brought to carry his father's remains back to Radnor was far too short and small for the task at hand, and Isaac was faced with the rather grisly possibility of openly transporting a cadaver across the countryside. Finally, in consultation with an old friend of his father's, Dr. James Wallace, a solution was agreed to that would not only solve the problem, it would also satisfy the disappointment of the locals in Erie who didn't want to lose their war hero.

> Isaac was faced with the rather grisly possibility of openly transporting a cadaver across the countryside.

That night, Isaac Wayne and Dr. Wallace (after drinking a sizable quantity of liquor to steel themselves for the task, I am sure) carefully dismembered the body, placed it in a large cauldron and boiled the general's body until they had separated the flesh from the bones!

They literally spent the evening boiling Mad.

The next morning, the good general's flesh and viscera (the "Mad Anthony" Wayne "soup" if you will) were reburied in his original grave in Erie along with his clothing. The bones and skull were given to Isaac and transported by wagon to Radnor where they were eventually reburied there in the family crypt.

Interestingly, a local legend still persists that on the trip to Radnor, Isaac somehow lost a few of the bones, and every

New Year's Day, "Mad Anthony" Wayne haunts the road, traveling back and forth between Erie and Radnor looking for his missing bones.

Actually, I'm not sure why the general should be so upset; most people in life think that it's impossible to be in two places at once. In death (and subsequent dual burial) "Mad Anthony" Wayne did just that.

General Anthony Wayne's son was boiling mad after finding out about his father's burial.

O, Say Can You Bail Me Out? The Birth of Our National Anthem

It was the War of 1812, a three-year war between the U.S. and Great Britain 30 years after the American Revolution, in which the mighty British Empire attempted to bloody the nose of their once colonial possession as the Americans fought in an equal fashion to resist it. Over the course of the war, the U.S. invaded Canada, and the British burned Washington, D.C., and the White House. Finally a peace treaty was signed in late 1814 that returned everything at issue to its prewar borders. Against this heated backdrop, our national anthem, "The Star Spangled Banner," was born.

Following the burning of Washington, D.C. and the White House, the British victoriously moved on to Baltimore and began besieging the city. A group of heroic American soldiers were holed up in Fort McHenry in Baltimore Harbor where the British lobbed cannon shells at them from their warships.

Back in Washington, D.C. several British soldiers had been victoriously getting drunk for several hours and looting whatever they could find in the city and surrounding area. A well-known Maryland resident named Dr. William Beanes had the beans to try and stop them and was, of course, immediately arrested and hauled off to the custody of the invading British forces.

Word of the good doctor's arrest made its way to local attorney and amateur poet Francis Scott Key, who was summoned to come to the aid of Dr. Beanes and see if he could get him bailed out of British custody.

Key made his way, not without some difficulty, to the British place of custody: onboard one of the British ships in the harbor.

For the next 24 hours or so, Francis Scott Key personally witnessed one of the key moments in American history. He did indeed secure the release of Dr. Beanes, but because he'd been amongst the British ships, they felt he might give information to American forces defending Fort McHenry. So they kept him as a "neutral" prisoner for the next 24 hours on his boat while they continued to bombard Fort McHenry with their cannons.

> By the dawn's early light: Francis Scott Key had a bird's-eye view of the U.S. flag flying at Fort McHenry in 1814 when he penned our national anthem.

By the dawn's early light, Francis Scott Key and everyone else saw the American flag still waving over the fort. The Americans had survived the onslaught of the British cannons and still held their position! Good time to write a poem while in enemy custody. And that's exactly what Francis Scott Key did. On the back of an envelope, he penned the poem that would become our national anthem.

Unable to dislodge the Americans from Fort McHenry, the British ships eventually pulled back and moved away from Baltimore Harbor. To the young nation of the United States, this was a great victory against the mighty British.

Key's poem "The Defense of Fort McHenry" was quickly published in newspapers across the nation and from the beginning was sung to the tune of an old British drinking song called "To Anacreon in Heaven." Someone gave it the more direct name of "The Star Spangled Banner," and it also famously became a marching song of northern troops in the Civil War. In 1931 it was made the U.S. national anthem.

Thanks to some drunken British soldiers, an American lawyer/poet and an old British drinking song, the United States has a song we can all watch someone forget the words to at the beginning of a baseball game.

It's actually a very interesting song. Most people only know the first verse, but check out the other verses for some particularly damning anti-British lyrics from ol' Francis that must have made sense to them in 1814.

As for our national anthem and how it came to be, I say, "Cheers!"

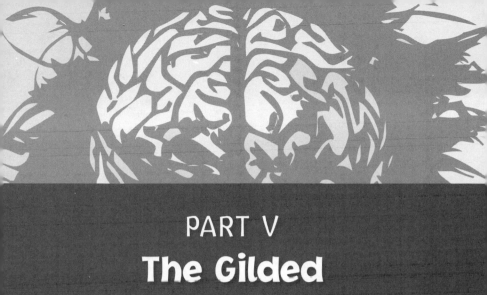

PART V
The Gilded Age

Having a Friend for Dinner

The group of 87 California-bound travelers known as the "Donner Party" is infamous for their attempted late-1840s trip across the Sierra Nevada Mountains, where they got caught by a series of massive snowstorms and where many of them resorted to cannibalism to survive. Of the 87 original members, 41 died and 46 survived. At least half of the survivors ate some of their fellow travelers to survive.

From November 1846 until April 1847, when the last survivor was rescued, this poor group of people had some of the worst luck in history as they encountered blizzard after blizzard, split up, then recombined, then split up again, all the while trying to find a way over the mountains between northern Nevada and California.

> Forty-six members of the Donner party survived, many of them having cannibalized their companions to do so.

Four separate rescue attempts were launched to find any survivors, and at each location of huddling, near-frozen survivors that the rescuers came across, there was evidence of cannibalism. At some locations evidence even suggested that members of the party, primarily Hispanic servants along for the journey, had been deliberately killed to be eaten.

None of the survivors was ever charged with a crime.

During an interview after the ordeal, one of the female survivors summed up the entire months-long horrific experience by warning, "Don't take 'shortcuts.'"

Indeed.

They Called Him "Handsome Frank," but Life Turned Ugly

The 14th president of the United States, Franklin Pierce, seemed to have been born into a charmed life. The son of the governor of New Hampshire, he studied law at Maine's Bowdoin College, married the daughter of the college's president, and, embarking on a career in politics, seemed destined for great things.

Called "Handsome Frank" by his friends, Pierce was charming and affable, and after time in the U.S. House of Representatives, he was elected to the Senate, also as a Democrat, where he was a devoted follower of the policies of the Democratic Party–hero and former President Andrew Jackson.

After resigning from politics for a few years, and a short military stint in the Mexican War, Pierce attended the Democratic presidential nominating convention in 1852. After an exhausting deadlock of 48 rounds of votes without a nominee (this was before the primary system), Pierce himself got the nomination as a compromise candidate along with the new nickname "Young Hickory" (a takeoff on Andrew Jackson's nickname "Old Hickory"). Winning the election handily over the Whig Party candidate, Winfield Scott, things were looking up, but they then began to take a turn for the worse for Handsome Frank.

It seems he had two nagging bits of baggage that proved to cause him the greatest worry and difficulty. One was his wife, Jane, and one was alcohol. His agoraphobic wife never liked their years in Washington, D.C., when Franklin had been a representative and a senator there, feeling the lifestyle contributed greatly to Franklin's heavy drinking and general dissolution. It was for her that Franklin had taken a leave of absence from politics and alcohol for a few years before his nomination and election as president. Jane saw only doom in the coming presidency of her husband, and she was ultimately proven right.

On the train trip from New Hampshire to Washington, D.C. in 1853, the Pierces' young (and only) child, 11-year-old Bennie, begged his parents to be able to leave the passenger compartment and to go up to the front section of the train for a better look at the engine. After letting the young boy do so,

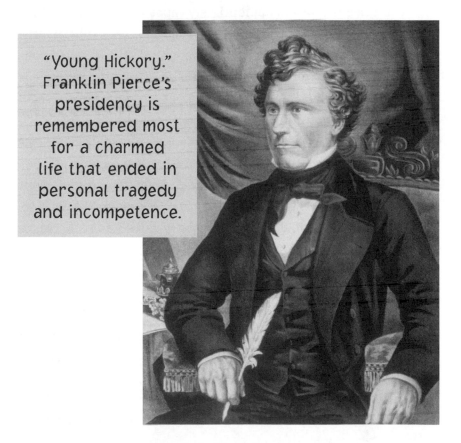

"Young Hickory." Franklin Pierce's presidency is remembered most for a charmed life that ended in personal tragedy and incompetence.

to the utter shock and horror of Franklin and Jane, the train derailed. While the Pierces themselves were unharmed in the crash, they saw their only son crushed to death right before their very eyes!

Mrs. Pierce was naturally devastated, inconsolable, and remained in mourning and melancholic for the rest of her life. This was the proof of the doom she had foreseen when her husband had won the election. The ensuing inauguration was a dark, dismal affair and was not even attended by Mrs. Pierce.

The sheer bleakness of the first sputtering steps of Pierce's executive tenure was appropriately capped by the death of his vice president, William Rufus de Vane King, from tuberculosis, less than a month after the inauguration! All this was the funereal preliminary setting for one of the most contentious periods in American history as the issue of slavery rose unswervingly to the forefront of U.S. political life.

On this most important and troubling of issues, Pierce was singularly and even grandly ineffectual. When he wasn't angering his fellow northerners with one decision, he was pissing off the southerners with another. The national corrosion of the slavery issue culminated most strikingly with the Kansas-Nebraska Act of 1854, concerning these two territories that wanted to join the Union as states.

This act repealed the Missouri Compromise of 1820, which had drawn boundaries on which states could be "free" and which could be "slave." Historically, this had resulted in a mathematically equalized admission process by which one free state joined the Union for every slave state, keeping the political balance of power. The new legislation, however, declared that the new state-to-be territories of Nebraska and Kansas would themselves decide "by popular vote" which way to go. The result was "Bleeding Kansas," a bloody, mindless free-for-all as pro-slavers and anti-slavers poured into Kansas to mercilessly influence the vote in their favor by force of murder and intimidation.

The combination of the brutal savagery of the conflict in Kansas and Pierce's inept handling of the crisis led directly to the formation of the Republican Party, the death of the Whig Party, and a bitter North/South split in the Democratic Party that would not heal for decades. When Pierce ran for reelection in 1856, he was denied renomination by his own party, the Democrats, the only time in history a president has been repudiated in this way by his own political party.

Instead of Pierce, James Buchanan got the Democratic nomination and went on to be president in 1857. But the split in the Democratic Party was too severe and Abraham Lincoln would become the first Republican president four years later in 1861, leading of course to the Civil War and the end of slavery in the U.S.

As for "Handsome Frank," he retired in defeat to his home in Concord, New Hampshire, with his inconsolable, invalid wife. Following her death a few years later, Pierce miserably declared, "There is nothing to do now but drink." Returning to the heavy-drinking ways of his earlier years, Pierce died of cirrhosis of the liver in 1869 at the age of 64, a broken, forgotten man. Hardly a fitting end for a president of the United States, who at one time seemed destined for the most handsome of destinies.

School of War

During the U.S. Civil War, 55 of the 60 major battles fought were commanded on both sides by graduates of West Point, the U.S. Military Academy. Many of the commanders knew the opposing commanders personally and had been classmates with them as well. With the same training, schooling, and esprit de corps, they now faced off against each other on American soil in the bloodiest, deadliest conflagration in American history. Without a doubt, I'm sure they hoped the other guys weren't paying attention during class!

Civil War Union Dead—400,000.

Civil War Confederacy Dead—300,000.

What a wonderful lesson.

Does This Ring a Bell?

Alexander Graham Bell is of course best known for his invention of the first working telephone. What is perhaps not so well known is that both Bell's mother and wife were deaf. His main and original interest in the science of acoustics and sound was to help the deaf hear and speak better. The telephone, the main communicating device so many of us hearing people use multiple times everyday, was invented for the deaf!

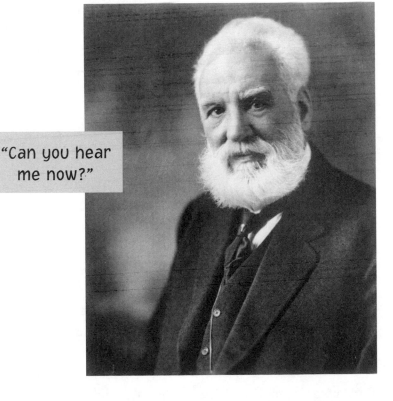

"Can you hear me now?"

President James A. Garfield and the Doctors Who Killed Him

Ohio native James Abram Garfield was the 20th president of the United States (1881) and sadly the second to be struck down by an assassin's bullet. A log cabin–born, self-made man who had served in the Civil War with distinction, he was also an ordained minister (our nation's one and only preacher prez) and, after serving eight terms as an Ohio congressman, was elected as a senator from the state.

In 1880 at the nominating convention for the Republican candidate for president in New York City, things forever changed for him. Garfield gave such an impressive speech introducing one of the three main nominees that when the votes were later split between the three, Garfield became the dark-horse pick for the nomination itself! Garfield tried in vain to have his name taken off the nomination, but it was too late. The man who had come in to introduce one of the candidates was now the candidate himself.

In the contentious election of November 1880, Garfield defeated the Democrats' Winfield Scott Hancock by

> Garfield and Guiteau: the reluctant president and his not-so-reluctant assassin.

less than 10,000 votes out of about 10 million cast. In part he used a biography written for him by none other than Horatio Alger, the author famous for his rags-to-riches stories. Sadly, we really can't say much about what kind of president Garfield would have made, as only four months into his term he was shot in the back at a Washington, D.C., train station by Charles Guiteau, a disgruntled office-seeker and religious wacko.

Guiteau had sent rambling speeches he had written to Garfield's staff during the campaign, and upon Garfield's election, his warped mind felt the proper reward was to be appointed U.S. Consul (Ambassador) to Paris. After showing up several times at the White House and demanding his appointment, the White House staff, who had never heard of him or his speeches, promptly threw him out and barred him from the premises. His revenge was to shoot Garfield twice while he waited for the train, once in the arm and once in the back, where the bullet could not be found. Guiteau was immediately arrested

and eventually executed by hanging almost a year later, after a dramatic and crazy trial.

Garfield was not so lucky. He lingered for two and a half months as various top doctors prodded and poked at the open bullet wound in his back without any sterilization (this was all before Louis Pasteur), even puncturing his lung at one juncture while probing for the elusive bullet! Arguably (and his autopsy supported this), Garfield more than likely would have lived if the doctors had just left the wound alone and allowed it to heal on its own. Instead, their fumbling efforts caused a small bullet hole to be extended into a 20-inch-long, open, festering wound and doomed our 20th president to a slow and painful death from infection and blood poisoning 80 days after he was shot.

One of the more hopeful measures utilized by those trying to help the stricken Garfield was an experimental metal detector invented by Alexander Graham Bell of telephone fame. His metal detector invention worked great in his workshop on a cow carcass shot with bullets, but it frustratingly went haywire every one of several times it was used on the ailing president. ("Turn him over. Let's try it again!") Only later after Garfield's death was it discovered that the bed on which the wounded president had lain had a metal bed frame, a recent cultural advance unexpected by the diligent Alexander Graham Bell, which thwarted his detector.

Sadly for President Garfield, though, his recovery was not to be. Transported to a beachside mansion on the New Jersey shore to give him some peace in his final days, Garfield died there on September 19, 1881, at the age of 49, and after only four months as president. The American people and the nation's newspapers had become so obsessed with the drawn-out passing of the president that the national outpouring of grief and mourning was surprisingly greater for Garfield than it had been for Abraham Lincoln 16 years before!

The nation mourned this common man who had survived the Civil War, who had never wanted the nomination that got him elected to the presidency, and who was shot by a disgruntled wacko he had never heard of. And who was obliged to die from an infected wound that would have healed on its own and never should have killed him. He is buried in Cleveland, Ohio.

Upon Garfield's death, Vice President Chester A. Arthur became our 21st president, presumably with better choice in doctors!

Garfield did leave behind one indication of his possible readiness to take a bite out of the government of which he had been the short-term president: he named his dog Veto!

The Four Non-Assassinated Dead Presidents

While a lot of attention in American history is naturally paid to those four U.S. presidents who were assassinated (Lincoln, Garfield, McKinley, and Kennedy), four other presidents also died in office before the end of their terms.

William Henry Harrison, our ninth president (1841), was a famous general renowned for his military victories against Native Americans and the British during the War of 1812, but he is even more famous today for the way he died. On Harrison's inauguration day in 1841, despite the fact that it was freezing cold and pouring down rain, Mr. Hardcore Indian Fighter wasn't gonna miss his party and insisted on giving a two-hour speech in the rain without wearing a hat or a warm coat. Catching pneumonia from this exposure, he died in the White House a mere one month after he had became president.

Zachary Taylor, our 12th president (1849–50), was a military hero of the Mexican War known as "Old Rough and Ready," who died suddenly and mysteriously in 1850 after only about one year as president. The official version was that Taylor had died after an allergic reaction from eating a dessert of cherries and cream! The president of the United States died from eating a bad dessert? Rumors persisted for decades that he had been poisoned,

> Long rain, short reign: William Henry Harrison is now known more for foolishly bringing on his own demise than for his distinguished military career or his month-long presidency.

but finally his body was exhumed in 1991, given an autopsy, and modern coroners officially concluded that he had not been poisoned.

Warren G. Harding, our 29th president (1921–23), was famous as the president who promised a "Return to Normalcy" following World War I and took office in 1921 at the beginning of the

Roaring Twenties. Sadly, Harding is now also famous for presiding over one of the most corrupt presidential administrations in U.S. history and for being a notorious womanizer who had at least two mistresses. He dropped dead only two years into his presidency, in 1923, in San Francisco from a heart attack on the way back from a visit to the U.S. frontier territory of Alaska. In the years that followed, there was much speculation that his wife had found out about his mistresses and had slowly poisoned him with arsenic until he dropped dead. Significantly, she demanded and was granted the right to bury her husband without an autopsy or any medical examination of the body. Hell hath no fury...

Franklin D. Roosevelt, our 32nd president (1933–45), served as U.S. chief executive longer than any other president in our history, and during two of its most difficult times: the Depression and World War II. Love him or hate him, the man was a leader who influenced the course of this nation like few others before or since. Elected to an unprecedented fourth term in 1944, he lived only about three months into that term before succumbing to a heart attack in 1945. Despite the fact that FDR had been in a wheelchair for decades as a result of polio, rumors abound of his own mistresses, including Lucy Mercer, who was supposedly with him when he died. With FDR's sudden death in 1945, it was left to new president Harry Truman to drop the atomic bomb in August of that year and end World War II.

One by rain, one by cherries, one by wife, one by life.

PART VI
A Century Turns

I Think That's a Bad Omen, Your New Highness

A lesson for all you would-be rulers out there...

Before the Russian Revolution of 1917, it was often the tradition to distribute free food, drinks, and gifts to the people of Moscow on a large scale when a new czar was crowned. And so it was on May 26, 1896, new czar Nicholas II's coronation day, that thousands of the people of Moscow and the surrounding suburbs were invited to celebrate the event at Khodynka Field with free beer, sausages, pastries, and gifts (simple enameled iron cups stamped with the royal seal).

Unfortunately, hundreds of thousands of the common people who had shown up for the freebies were streaming toward the giveaway stands as a rumor swept the crowd that there wasn't going to be enough for everyone. The resulting confusion and pushing and shoving culminated in a tragic stampede that left as many as 2,000 people crushed to death!

The czar and czarina wanted to go out into the people and comfort them during this horrible tragedy, but unfortunately they acquiesced to the wishes of their advisors and instead attended a lavish coronation ball given for them by the French embassy. The seemingly callous disregard of the czar for his fallen subjects added insult to injury. The blood on the ground of the field was seen as a terrible omen for the coming reign of the unfeeling, insensitive czar and his family.

Indeed, Czar Nicholas II seemed hard-pressed and ill-prepared to handle the administration of the vast and crumbling Russian Empire in the years that were to come. The disastrous Russo-Japanese War of 1904–5 was followed by the equally

Czar Trek, the Doomed Generation: Russan czar Nicholas II was ushered into his reign under less-than-ideal circumstances.

ill-fated Russian failure in World War I and capped by the ultimate crushing defeat, the forced abdication of the monarchy as a result of the Russian Revolution of 1917. A prisoner of the Bolshevik communist revolutionaries for several months, the czar and his entire household (him, his wife, their son, their four daughters, and a few faithful servants) were finally brutally murdered in cold blood in July 1918.

Not surprisingly, the 1896 coronation souvenirs for the common people of Moscow, the beer-drinking containers now often called the "Cup of Sorrows," are exceedingly rare and almost impossible to find in near-perfect condition. These tragic beer-mug memorials of the coronation of Nicholas II serve as a reminder that "Ya shoulda gone out and comforted the common people, czar boy!"

The Country That Moved from One Continent to Another

So you wanna get a canal built? Sometimes it takes moving a country to another continent. With help from the United States, the strategic region of Panama gained independence from Colombia in 1903. The problem for geographers was, until then, Panama was a part of Colombia, and Colombia was traditionally considered the northernmost nation in South America.

After independence in 1903, geographers "moved" Panama from South America to Central America, which is, of course, part of North America.

Hey, John! This Play Is a Riot!

After a few plays of minor success, an early 20th-century Irish playwright finally had a major hit...in the face!

In 1907, performances of John Millington Synge's new play *The Playboy of the Western World* provoked riots in his native Dublin and later in the United States as well. The play, a rural comedy about a mysterious stranger who shows up at a bar one night and tells a tale about killing his own father, apparently provoked the rage of the Irish attendees in both nations because it dared show the lives of regular Irish people with all their faults, feelings, and foibles.

To the nationalistic Irish of the early 20th century, forever at odds with their English overlords, any depiction of the Irish as anything less than noble, valiant heroes fighting forever against oppression was tantamount to treason. While the riots in Dublin and the U.S. amounted to little more than yelling and shoving and shouting down the actors, Synge himself at one performance had to finally stand on stage and shout down the rioters in the name of his art, to the point that finally, over time the protests subsided. Now that's a play!

The fightin' and writin' Irish: John Millington Synge's 1907 play sparked riots on both sides of the Atlantic.

Gregory Peck
starred in a
1946 production
of Synge's
controversial
1907 work.

Hey, Igor! This Ballet Is a Riot!

In the late 20th century and early 21st century, we've all unfortunately heard about crazy, riotous behavior at rock concerts and rap-music concerts, etc. But can you believe that people actually violently rioted at a ballet performance in 1913?

Many people date the birth of modern music to the premiere of the ballet *The Rite of Spring* in May 1913 at the Champs Elysées Theater in Paris. Performed to the music of the Russian composer Igor Stravinsky and the choreography of Vaslav Nijinsky, *The Rite of Spring* was no ordinary genteel ballet like the others of its time that the populace had come to expect.

Instead, the work is a depiction of pre-Christian pagan times in Russia and culminates in a human sacrifice! The work starts innocently enough with some ceremonial dancing and nature rituals, but as it moves ever more certainly to the ritual blood sacrifice, the music and the dancing build and build and build to a harsh and brutal crescendo that sent the Paris crowd into shocked and outraged hysterics!

How dare someone depict us civilized human beings as nothing more than bloodthirsty savage beasts! As the crowd stood and started yelling and screaming at this affront to their sensitive natures, a few started yelling back in support of the work. The crowd quickly got out of hand as the insulted audience members first started jostling with the defenders of the work and then outright fighting with them.

The audience was so shocked and scandalized by what they had seen and heard that they literally began to attack the dancers and the musicians and to tear down the theater itself! All in their top hats and tuxedos and fashionable ladies' gowns and furs!

One account of the incident reported that Stravinsky and others had to escape out a back window of the theater to get away from the enraged crowd as its bloodlust raged. Finally, the police had to be called in to prevent the audience from further destroying and literally burning down the theater. At a classical-music ballet performance in 1913!

Classical rocks! Composer Igor Stravinsky changed the face and scope of modern music for all time.

One thing is for sure, by breaking the musical rules of his time, Stravinsky took classical music into the modern age and influenced many other branches of the arts in his audacity and willingness to create the opposite of his audience's expectations, by pushing the musical limits in a way that hadn't been done before.

Some have called *The Rite of Spring* the greatest musical composition of the 20th century. At the very least, it was undoubtedly one of the most influential. With his brutal, dissonant, violent music, Stravinsky managed to shock his audience out of their complacency to the point that against their "refined and genteel natures," they themselves actually descended into barbaric, pagan destructive behavior of their own in response!

Stravinsky went on to continue as one of the most influential composers of his time, but none of his subsequent works had quite the same impact as this one. Sadly, as 1913 turned into 1914, the world plunged into a pagan, blood-sacrificing ritual of madness of its own that today we call World War I.

Just Couldn't Ask for Directions, Eh, Franz?

I n Sarajevo, Bosnia, in June 1914, Archduke Franz Ferdinand, the heir to the throne of the Austro-Hungarian empire, and his wife were visiting the Austrian-controlled territory of Bosnia. Pan-Serbian nationalists in Bosnia and next door in Serbia had recently doubled the size of their territory in the Balkan Wars at the expense of the Ottoman Turks. Now they were hoping to add Bosnia to that expansion, not kowtow to a new imperial overlord.

Having learned of his visit ahead of time, a group of Bosnian Serb assassins allied with shadowy militant nationalist groups called "The Black Hand" and "Young Bosnia!" awaited the Archduke in Sarajevo with bombs and guns.

> Miraculously, the Archduke batted the bomb away from himself and his wife...

As the Archduke's caravan wound its way through the city and the crowds, the first assassin struck, throwing a bomb at the Archduke's car. Miraculously, the Archduke batted the bomb away from himself and his wife, saving them, but it exploded near some of his men, several of whom were wounded. But the attack had been foiled.

As the police and soldiers swept in on the crowd, the assassins panicked and fled. Some were immediately captured, one tried to commit suicide, ashamed of his failure, and one, Gavrilo Princip, wandered aimlessly away from the scene, not sure what to do next. He nervously hid in a restaurant.

Sometime later, after the situation was secure and his other duties completed, the Archduke insisted on visiting his wounded men. His security team advised against it, but the Archduke was insistent. Unfamiliar with the Sarajevo streets, his driver took a wrong turn on the way to the hospital and pulled the car directly up in front of the restaurant where Gavrilo Princip, one of the assassins from earlier, was presumably drowning his sorrows at his failure!

Directly in front of where he was sitting was the Archduke's car, stopped, and with little or no protection!

Seizing his opportunity, Gavrilo leapt from his seat, raced outside, and shot the Archduke and his wife dead from point-blank range. He was then almost immediately captured. (He died in prison two years later.)

After all the protection and even a miraculous first escape from an assassin's bomb, the Archduke and his wife pulled up unprotected, right in front of their assassin. And all because a man wouldn't ask for directions?

The result of the Archduke's death was the start of World War I a few weeks later.

Woodrow Wilson: 28th President, Nobel Prize Winner, and Racist

On any list of favorite U.S. presidents, whether it is by laymen or historians, inevitably names like Franklin D. Roosevelt, Abraham Lincoln, John F. Kennedy, and even perhaps Ronald Reagan will appear. Alongside these fabled names, within the top 10 can usually be found the name of Woodrow Wilson, the Virginian who was also president of Princeton University before becoming president of the U.S. in 1913. He was the man who led America and the Allies to victory in World War I and laid the groundwork for the League of Nations, the forerunner of the modern United Nations. Sounds like a pretty honorable guy, right? Wrong! Dead wrong.

Unbeknownst to most Americans is the fact that Woodrow Wilson, Democrat, 28th president of the United States, and winner of the 1919 Nobel Peace Prize was a dyed-in-the-wool racist and white supremacist!

A few examples of the character of the man:

The first movie ever shown in the White House was the notoriously racist silent film *Birth of a Nation* in 1915. In a nutshell, the film (based on the book *The Clansman* by Thomas Dixon, a personal friend of Woodrow Wilson's) tells the story of how the Ku Klux Klan "saves" the South following the Civil War from the evil plundering of northern carpetbaggers and the criminal activities of lecherous and violent freed blacks. By some accounts, the film is even credited with reviving the Klan in modern times after it had fallen defunct around 1871. (The modern Klan was reconstituted in 1915, the same year *Birth of a Nation* came out.) Well, President Woodrow Wilson arranged the

showing of the film at the White House and the Supreme Court and insisted that prominent and powerful politicians of both parties attend the screenings! After viewing the film Wilson described it as "history written with lightning" and declared that the film "would be shocking! If it weren't so true!"

Another example of Wilson's contempt for African Americans, whom he and his wife often openly called "darkies," is the fact that in two terms as president (eight years), he rarely met with prominent black political and business leaders. One such occasion was when Wilson met with the prominent black newspaper publisher William Monroe Trotter. Trotter had requested the meeting to ask the president about moves he had made to re-segregate part of the government. To the eternal shame of our 28th president, Wilson had the unbridled audacity to basically tell Trotter to his face that American blacks should be satisfied and content with their second-class status in U.S. society because, as America was the number-one country in the world, being a second-class citizen here was better than they could ever hope for anywhere else! When Trotter incredulously asked Wilson if he was serious in spouting such ridiculous racist hokum, Wilson flew into a rage and had Trotter thrown out of the White House.

> Woodrow Wilson's endorsement of the racist film *Birth of a nation* may have revived the Ku Klux Klan.

Through acts like this one and many others, Wilson's presidency could conceivably be said to have set back black participation in mainstream American politics for years to come.

This is the man whom some historians and others, apparently ignorant of his real character, routinely place near the top of lists of "Favorite American Presidents," primarily for the actions he took during World War I and the years immediately after. But by any stretch of the imagination, whatever your political party or persuasion, Woodrow Wilson should be placed dead last on any list of favorite U.S. presidents.

PART VII
Modern Times

Put a Ford in Your Racism

The American industrialist Henry Ford is best known for his pioneering work in the automobile industry, including his innovative use of assembly line production. The man is practically synonymous with American industrial might and ingenuity, all wrapped up in the package of a self-made success. What is perhaps not so well-known about the man is that he was also a raging racist and anti-Semite of epic proportions.

In a written work called *The International Jew*, published in installments in Henry Ford's own newspaper, *The Dearborn Independent*, Ford laid out the case and the blame for the Jews being responsible for everything from communism, gambling, jazz, and illegal liquor to vice and corruption of every imaginable variety. A firm believer in *The Protocols of Zion* (a notorious forgery that purported to reveal a great Jewish plot to take over the world), Ford was determined to reveal this great Jewish conspiracy to the world.

While it's hard to say definitively how much Ford directly supported the Nazis, there is no doubt that with works like *The International Jew*, he at least sympathized with their anti-Semitic, Jew-hating ideology. How many young American men (Jewish, Christian, and otherwise) died in World War II because this supposed paragon of American values had spewed his Nazi-like hate and support of anti-Semitism?

Interestingly enough, Henry Ford, shining symbol of American democracy and free enterprise, is praised glowingly by name in Adolf Hitler's *Mein Kampf*. Also, in 1938, one year before the invasion of Poland and the start of World War II, when the

Henry Ford was the innovator
of modern American industry—
and an old-fashioned racist.

intents of Nazi Germany were more than clear, Ford accepted the Grand Cross of the German Eagle, the highest accolade bestowed by the Nazis on non-Germans. Henry Ford, the man, had a cracked engine block for a brain and a flat tire for a soul.

The thing that always blows my mind about all these take-over-the-world conspiracy theories (whether it be about the Jews, the Freemasons, the Boy Scouts, or whoever) is that these "evil forces" are always so powerful and so manipulative behind the scenes for so very, very long, yet somehow they never seem to complete the deed!

There's Just One Little Flaw in Your Plan, Mr. Maginot

Following World War I, the French Minister of War, André Maginot, advocated staunch military preparedness against France's age-old enemy Germany by proposing the construction of a huge defensive line that would stretch for thousands of miles along the border between the two nations. The resulting system of fortifications (that ultimately would bear the minister of war's name as the Maginot Line) stretched from Switzerland to Belgium along France's eastern border with Germany. It cost billions of

> ...the Maginot Line had not been completed in a critical way.

francs to build, utilized tons upon tons of concrete, and incorporated bunkers, machine guns, tank traps, heavy artillery, and miles of underground tunnels and facilities to be utilized by thousands of soldiers in the event of an attempted invasion from Germany.

There was only one problem with this plan.

When World War II broke out in 1939, the Maginot Line had not been completed in a critical way. A few years earlier in 1936, Belgium had pulled out of a military treaty with France and declared neutrality in an effort to appease the obvious growing military might of a rearming Germany. As a result, the construction of the Maginot Line's massive fortifications was not carried northward out of France into Belgium's Ardennes Forest. When the Nazis moved westward to invade France in early 1940, all they had to do was bypass the massive Maginot Line and all its impressive weaponry and manpower simply by going north through Belgium and around and behind the Maginot Line! And that's exactly what they did.

In only a matter of days the Germans did indeed confront the mighty Maginot Line, but from behind! So confident had the French been of the direction of the German attack that some of their heavy artillery only pointed east toward Germany! Many of their biggest guns couldn't even be swiveled around to face the advancing Germans who were basically coming in the Maginot Line's back door. It was a horrible, crushing defeat for the French, and they paid dearly for it.

A few remaining French soldiers attempted to make a last stand underground in the Maginot Line's tunnels, but the Germans merely brought in bulldozers and sealed all the entrances and air ducts of the underground areas, effectively entombing the courageous soldiers.

Several years after the war ended in 1945, something miraculous happened. A construction crew was clearing part of the line to make way for a new road, and out from an underground tunnel walked half a dozen French soldiers who had survived underground all that time. They had survived underground for more than seven years!

In that time they endlessly searched and dug for a way out and had watched many of their companions either die from exposure, madness, disease, or suicide. Somehow they managed to survive on the food supplies stored underground, as well as an amply stocked wine cellar.

They were heroes to the French people, but I'm sure if they had one bit of advice for France's postwar leaders it would be, "Watch your back, you goofs! If you're gonna build a defensive wall, make sure the enemy can't just bypass it by coming in the back door!"

Dr. Albert Hofmann: LSD Inventor and User

Working for Sandoz Laboratories in the 1930s, Swiss biochemist Albert Hofmann was researching the ingredients in medicinal plants in the hopes of synthesizing any of their active components. Working with ergot alkaloids one evening, he felt a bit dizzy and went home where he had strange dreams while still awake. Believing he'd accidentally ingested something from his work, he tried again on purpose a few days later. But because he had no idea of the potency of the active ingredients he was ingesting, he ended up taking the equivalent of five hits of "acid" his very first time! For those who don't know, that's a lot. Especially your first time.

A trip to the lab: Dr. Albert Hofmann accidentally discovered LSD, but he quite intentionally continued to take it afterward.

As it all hit him while riding home on his bicycle, he began flying mentally into a phantasmagoric LSD world for the first time by anyone in history. Once home, he spent hours in panic and fear, thinking he was going insane or that he would die. Finally past peaking, he relaxed and finished his wild ride calmly and pleasantly.

But afterwards, the profundity of the experience was not lost on Dr. Hofmann. He was of course convinced he'd synthesized an important compound from the ergot alkaloids, lysergic acid diethylamide. Or as it's known by the abbreviation of its German name, *LSD*, from *Lyserg-Säure-Diäthylamid*.

Dr. Hofmann reportedly took LSD many, many more times in the decades to come and in January 2007 turned 101 years old with his mind as sharp as ever. Trippy!

The Dictator and the Duke

A recent biography of the legendary actor, *John Wayne: The Man behind the Myth,* by British author Michael Munn reveals that Soviet dictator Joseph Stalin was so angered by John Wayne's anti-communism stances and statements that he actually plotted to murder the American movie star. Several attempts in the 1940s and '50s included an effort by two KGB operatives posing as FBI agents to kill him at his offices in Burbank on the Warner Bros. lot. But the plot was uncovered and the would-be assassins arrested.

Luckily for the Duke, with Stalin's death in 1953, Soviet power shifted to Nikita Khrushchev and, as he was a big fan of the Duke and his movies, he promptly canceled the assassination plots. Thanks, pilgrim!

Have You Checked the Mailbox?

In 1958 Harry Winston of Tiffany's Diamonds sent the stunning 44.5 carat, sapphire-blue "Hope Diamond," one of the most famous and valuable gems in the world, from his offices in New York City to the Smithsonian Institution in Washington, D.C. by regular U.S. mail! It was inside a simple brown package with the museum's address on it, and it traveled through regular mail to its destination successfully. Winston did, however, have the gem insured before the mailing for $2 million.

He Coulda Killed Him with a Coke Bottle

In the past 40 years there has been widespread belief in conspiracy theories concerning Lee Harvey Oswald and the assassination of JFK in 1963. While many of them are fascinating and compelling, there is a simple alternative if you want to investigate the truth for yourself.

Go to Dealey Plaza in Dallas, Texas, the site of the assassination.

You can go to Dallas and walk around the assassination site, the School Book Depository, the Grassy Knoll, etc.; don't worry, you won't be intrusive. It's all been turned into a weird carnival/national historic shrine—you can even pay to ride in a convertible limousine on JFK's route, equipped with a tape recording of all the sounds from that day. As you pass over the large *X* painted in the road where the fatal bullets hit our 35th president, you'll hear gunfire on the tape!

All this is mindblowing enough, but one thing becomes

The infamous grassy knoll in Dallas.

painfully troublesome when you stand next to the School Book Depository and look over at the big *X* in the road—it's only about 50 feet away.

Shockingly, it's so close it seems as if you or I or any other reasonably able person could have potentially done it, never mind an ex-marine sharpshooter. Admittedly, Lee Harvey Oswald was allegedly shooting from the sixth-floor window, but even from there it's so close one wonders if Lee Harvey Oswald could have killed JFK with an accurately thrown Coke bottle!

And the Grassy Knoll? Where supposedly another shot could have come from? When you look at the footage and graphs and photos on JFK conspiracy TV shows, movies, etc., it looks far away. But the truth is, it's only a few yards farther down the street from the Depository. It's hard to believe you could pop open a can of beer at that spot without half the people in the Plaza hearing you, let alone shoot off a gun.

There are real conspiracies and there are real mysteries that will never be solved, but when the actual physical spaces of the Dealey Plaza assassination site are looked at from the ground, in person, it seems as though the real conspiracy to a straight-forward observer would have been if Lee Harvey Oswald had missed.

One last thought: if there was any shred of real evidence to the JFK conspiracy theories, wouldn't the Kennedy family, one of the most powerful, wealthy, and influential families in U.S. history, have done absolutely anything possible in the last 40-plus years to expose the true killers and conspirators? To this day they have not challenged the official version of events. At least not publicly.

But somehow, of course, they could be in on it, too!

Go Ahead,
Make My Police Department

In 1972 the Manila Police Department in the Philippines contacted Warner Bros. for a copy of the Clint Eastwood movie *Dirty Harry* to use as a police procedure training tape. It's unknown if Warner Bros. ever sent them a copy.

Tromso, Norway:
A Nice Place to Get a Cold Beer

At 250 miles north of the Arctic Circle, Tromso, Norway, is home to the world's northernmost university and the world's northernmost brewery.

Coincidence? I think not!

No problem with the brewskis staying cold in Tromso!

The .44 caliber Derringer pistol that John Wilkes Booth used in 1865 to kill President Abraham Lincoln at Ford's Theater is held by the Department of the Interior in Washington, D.C.

The James A. Garfield National Historic Site in Ohio believes that the British Bull Dog .44 caliber, five-chambered revolver with a fancy grip that Charles Guiteau used to kill President Garfield in 1881 is lost, its whereabouts unknown.

The pistol used by Leon Czolgosz to assassinate President William McKinley in Buffalo, New York, in 1901, an Iver-Johnson "Safety Automatic" revolver in .32 S&W caliber, is held by the Buffalo & Erie County Historical Society in Buffalo, New York.

The Mannlicher-Carcano rifle used by Lee Harvey Oswald to kill President John F. Kennedy in 1963 in Dallas is in the possession of the National Archives and Records Administration in Washington, D.C.

Jack Ruby's gun that he used to kill Oswald, a Colt Cobra .38 Special revolver, was sold in 1991 for $220,000 to a New Jersey gun collector, but its whereabouts are uncertain as it remains tied up in a court case.

And John Hinckley's gun? A Rohm RG-14 revolver in .22LR caliber with a 1$\frac{7}{8}$ inch barrel, which he used to try to kill President Ronald Reagan in 1981? Whereabouts unknown. Possibly in the possession of the Washington, D.C. court system.

The power of mail order: The Mannlicher-Carcano rifle used by Lee Harvey Oswald to kill President John F. Kennedy.

115

PART VIII
Unusual Origins and Inventive Minds

You've Got the Smile of a Twenty-Year-Old!

From out of the mouths of babes come...teeth?

The Battle of Waterloo in Belgium in 1815 was, of course, Napoleon's final defeat, but it was also an absolute boon to the practice of dentistry at the time. While some think that people like George Washington had wooden false teeth, the truth is that most people who needed them at the time and could afford them used elephant, hippo, and other types of animal ivory. In fact some of the best false teeth and dentures of the time that you could get were used human teeth.

In the wake of the great battles of the late 18th century and early 19th century, enterprising amateur dentists would prowl the battlefields, clandestinely ripping out and collecting the teeth and jaws of the dead soldiers on both sides before the bodies were collected for burial!

The Battle of Waterloo, between Napoleon's French forces and a combined British and Prussian force near the small village of Waterloo in Belgium, resulted in the deaths of close to 50,000 troops in a single day. This was indeed the high-water mark for these dental thieves, and they took full advantage of it.

You can't really blame the dentists. Aside from the teeth of dead soldiers, the only human teeth available for use in dentures were those taken from condemned prisoners and dead homeless people, usually not to be considered a primary source of young, vibrant, healthy teeth. And so from the mouths of the fallen soldiers, these healthy young teeth found their way into the mouths of the living where it became quite fashionable

The Battle of Waterloo: nearly 50,000 deaths—and countless sets of dentures.

to be known that you were chomping away with what became known as your "Waterloo Teeth."

It gives new meaning to the compliment that someone might have paid you that, "You've got the smile of a 20-year-old!"

As a matter of fact, I do!

Alfred Nobel: I'm Just Dead

Everyone knows that Alfred Nobel invented dynamite and also bankrolled the Nobel Prizes, but the connection between the two is not as well known. In the 1800s, Nobel was a prominent member of a Swedish family that owned chemical factories. Many of the company's products were explosives used in mining and construction. One of the most important and most dangerous was nitroglycerin. And deadly, too. Many had died in the handling of "nitro," including his brother. Young Alfred discovered a way to add the nitro to an inert mineral substance that made it much easier to transport and use. He called it dynamite, and as a result the family company made millions. Alfred himself also had the great personal satisfaction of knowing he had saved countless lives.

> Alfred was to be forever remembered as "the Merchant of Death."

Many years later, when Nobel was a man in his grey years, he was staying in Paris and picked up the morning paper to read. There amongst the pages was a listing that turned his blood cold: "The Merchant of Death Is Dead—Alfred Nobel—Inventor of Dynamite—Dead at Age 75." It was his obituary! Unbeknownst to Alfred, another of his brothers had died the day before, but in some journalistic confusion, it had been reported that Alfred himself had died, and so newspapers in Paris were running his obituary instead. Stunned beyond belief and still very much alive, Alfred read this short accounting of the sum total of his life.

Therein, Alfred Nobel was described as the guy who had invented dynamite, that infernal invention that had led to so many deaths in wars, accidents, and civil strife. In the years since its invention, yes, there had been other, non-industrial applications of dynamite, but what about all the many lives that had been saved by its use? What about the great changes for the better that had been wrought by the intelligent, controlled use of dynamite? As well as all the other chemical enhancements to human life and living that Nobel's work and the work of his family's company had led to? All for naught. He was to be forever remembered as "the guy who invented dynamite," one of the best ways to kill and destroy more efficiently.

Using the telegraph, Alfred learned of his brother's death, surmised the mix-up that had happened, and endeavored on a new course of action in his final years to change the way that he would be remembered by history.

The result was to endow the prestigious Nobel Prizes, awards given out each year to recognize and finance the world's greatest minds and achievements in fields ranging from chemistry and biology to literature and peace.

And all because he got to read his own obituary while he was still alive! Obviously, he didn't like the way his existence had been summed up, and he resolved to change it. When he really died a few years later, his obituary discussed in equal measure his invention of dynamite and his endowment of the Nobel Prizes.

And how will you be remembered?

A Lack of Patients Gives the World Its Greatest Fictional Detective

Sir Arthur Conan Doyle is of course best known as the literary creator of the famous detective Sherlock Holmes. What is less well known are the facts behind the creation.

Born in Edinburgh in 1859, Doyle earned a degree in medicine from the University of Edinburgh and, after a short period as a ship's doctor on a trip to West Africa, set up his medical practice in Plymouth, the famous sailing town of southwest England.

Unfortunately, things did not go well for the young doctor. A significant lack of patients caused Doyle to return to one of his youthful hobbies of writing stories to pass the time. It was these early endeavors that would lay the groundwork for what was to come. After moving his practice to Portsmouth, Doyle began his writing in earnest, and in 1887 his first significant work, "A Study in Scarlet," appeared in *Beeton's Christmas Annual*. The story featured the first appearance of Sherlock Holmes. With its depiction of the brilliant, quirky detective and his sidekick Dr. Watson, it was an instant hit.

The rest, as they say, is history. Doyle went on to write over 50 short stories and four novels featuring his master detective, who incidentally was based in large measure on one of his professors from medical school at the University of Edinburgh. At one point Doyle even killed off Sherlock Holmes out of sheer narrative exhaustion, but the public outcry forced him to bring him back to life and continue with more adventures.

Doyle also wrote many science-fiction stories, including *The Lost World*, numerous historical novels, plays, romances, poetry, and nonfiction. He also twice ran for parliament, but despite decent showings in the polls lost both times. In 1902 he was knighted, not for his fictional literary output, but instead for an essay he wrote in support of Britain's highly unpopular military campaigns during the Boer War in southern Africa. In his later years he also became highly interested in spiritualism and fairies, especially after the death of his son Kingsley Doyle in World War I.

> The ubiquitous Sherlock Holmes was originally called Sherringford Hope.

The remarkable question is, what would have happened had Doyle had plenty of patients when he initially set up his medical practice all those years ago? If Doyle's time had been spent pursuing his chosen profession, would the world have received one of its most famous, amazing, and enduring characters? The one-of-a-kind master detective Sherlock Holmes? Probably not.

Final note: he didn't need hope. The original name Arthur Conan Doyle chose for the character of his masterful detective was Sherringford Hope. With a few minor adjustments to the first name and changing the last name to match that of Doyle's favorite American writer, Oliver Wendell Holmes, the one and only Sherlock Holmes was born.

Forget the Movement, This Game Is Fun!

The board game today known as *Monopoly* began in 1904 among a group of working-class anti-capitalists called the Georgists, who originally called it "The Landlord's Game." As invented by them, they thought the game would demonstrate the inherent and immoral inequality between big-money landowners and poor, working-class renters.

The funny thing is, the movement that spawned *Monopoly* is gone and forgotten, but its game lives on. Not as a testament to owner/renter dynamics and a better understanding of social inequalities, but rather as a straight-ahead, no-holds-barred, winner-take-all contest to see who can crowd all the others out and own everything!

SPAM! SPAM! SPAM! SPAM! SPAM! The Wonder Meat

SPAM luncheon meat was first introduced in 1937 by the Hormel Company of Austin, Minnesota. And while it has been lampooned in a memorable Monty Python sketch, which featured a restaurant where almost every menu item included SPAM, and has also ingloriously lent its name to the vast waves of hated and unsolicited junk email in the age of the Internet, the product itself has a distinguished and intriguing history.

SPAM (SPiced hAM), was named SPAM following a contest in the 1930s and was first introduced to American grocery shelves in 1937. While selling successfully as a "miracle meat" that could be served anytime, it was the advent of World War II when SPAM really began to flex its muscles. As SPAM didn't need to be refrigerated, it was perfect for soldiers in war zones and wasn't rationed the way beef was, quickly making it a major staple of the American diet both at home and on the battlefield during those years.

SPAM was also the national sponsor of the George Burns and Gracie Allen radio show in the 1940s, and to help them pitch SPAM over the airwaves, they were joined by a character named Spammy the Pig. Due to meat shortages brought on by food rationing during World War II, the state of Hawaii began to eat SPAM like it was going out of style and today consumes more SPAM per capita than any other state, serving it up in such local favorites as SPAM Musubi.

In one of his many courageous radio broadcasts from London in 1942, Edward R. Murrow related that, "Although the Christmas table will not be lavish, there will be SPAM for everyone."

Indeed, in the 1960s, Soviet leader Nikita Khrushchev declared, "Without SPAM we would not have been able to feed our army" during World War II. Truly a miraculous product that usually doesn't get the credit it deserves.

Today the Hormel Corporation produces over 400 cans of SPAM a minute, yearly sales are somewhere in the 140 million range, and in 2002 it produced its six billionth can. You can also today find SPAM varieties like "Smoke Flavored," "Less Sodium," and "SPAM Lite." There is even a SPAM museum in the city of Austin, Minnesota, that's open to the visiting public,

SPAM: The wonder meat that helped win World War II.

and where the exciting and varied production and history of SPAM is forever enshrined.

Surprisingly, today the Hormel Corporation does not object to the use of the word *spam* for unsolicited emails, but instead asks only that if you use the word SPAM to refer to their product, use it in all capital letters (SPAM) and follow it with the words *luncheon meat*. As for that damn dreaded spam that's overflowing your email's inbox as you read this, blame either a man named Gary Thuerk or a man named Lawrence Canter. Both have been "credited" with introducing this kind of spam into our homes and places of business.

Better yet, instead of crediting them, maybe you could throw a can of SPAM luncheon meat at them!

PART IX

Say What? The Birth of Words and Phrases

French Frogs
Frolicking Frivolously

From about AD 400 to AD 800, as the historic ethnic group known as the Franks unified parts of Western Europe under the Merovingian dynasty and finally under Charlemagne and his heirs to create the nation of France, one of the royal symbols depicted on their coat of arms was three golden toads. Hence the origin of the French being known (somewhat derisively) as the frogs? Perhaps...

"Who're you calling a toad?"

You're Such a Dunce! But Don't Be Offended

In modern usage, the term *dunce* is used to denote sort of a klutzy, unintelligent person, complete with the ever-present dunce hat. Ironically, the word comes from the name of John Duns Scotus, a 13th-century Scottish theologian and philosopher who taught at Oxford and Cambridge universities and also in Paris. The irony stems from the fact that he was probably one of the smartest humans of his time, and many credit him with laying the foundation for separating science and philosophy from theology and religion in Western culture. How did this genius lend his name to a term for goofs and simpletons?

The answer lies in the fact that in his day his followers and students were often called "dunses," with the connotation that they were the equivalent of modern-day intelligent egg-heads or really smart nerds like their famous teacher. Over the intervening seven centuries, the meaning shifted from meaning smart geeks to meaning people stubbornly stuck in their ways of thinking and finally to meaning dimwits or numbskulls. That is how, ironically, one of the most important and smartest humans of all time lends his name to a term for morons.

Not very smart!

Somewhere, John Duns Scotus is rolling over in his grave.

Have a Drink on Me!
The Pickling of Lord Horatio Nelson

The British Admiral Lord Horatio Nelson is generally considered one of the greatest naval heroes in history. His defeat of a combined French and Spanish fleet at the naval Battle of Trafalgar in 1805 prevented a French invasion of Great Britain by Napoleon and ensured British dominance of the seas for the next 100 years.

Sadly for Lord Nelson, he himself did not survive his greatest victory, dying from a sniper's bullet shortly before the very end of the battle.

While many sailors killed in naval battles were buried at sea, such was not to be with the great hero. Instead, Lord Nelson's body was immersed in a cask of alcohol to preserve it

for the journey back to England. Arriving back in Great Britain, it was discovered that the liquid in Lord Nelson's cask was at a much lower level than could be accounted for by evaporation or other causes alone.

Apparently, sailors had been sneaking in and drinking the booze surrounding the body of the dead Nelson, leading to the slang term still used by the British Navy today of "tapping the admiral" to refer to taking an illicit drink onboard ship!

> British Admiral Lord Horatio Nelson was struck down at the naval Battle of Trafalgar, but that didn't stop his sailors from drinking to his health!

Today Nelson is buried in London's St. Paul's Cathedral and is further memorialized by his famous namesake column that towers over Trafalgar Square.

I'm sure he would say to one and all who gaze up at his column, "Have a drink on me!"

Women and Children First! The Birth of a Soggy, Noble Tradition

In February 1852, the British ship HMS *Birkenhead* struck a sunken rock off the coast of Africa and rapidly began to sink. No one knows exactly how it happened, but that night, as the ship sank and its passengers scrambled for their lives into the available lifeboats, there began the great noble sea tradition of "women and children first." The gallant sailors and passengers of the *Birkenhead* made sure that all available places in the lifeboats were filled by the women and children passengers before any man stepped into them. Of the approximately 650 passengers onboard, more than 400 men drowned; all the women and children survived.

All hail the brave heroes of the HMS *Birkenhead*, who gave the world the great naval tradition of "women and children first."

The Butler Did It! Thanks to Author Mary Roberts Rinehart

Called the American Agatha Christie, Mary Roberts Rinehart (1876–1958) was a nurse who began writing stories around 1903 in an effort to make some extra money and published her first mystery novel, *The Circular Staircase,* in 1908. It was an instant hit and led to a series of mysteries, plays, novels, and various other successful publications throughout her life. She also worked as a war correspondent for *The Saturday Evening Post* during the First World War on the French and Belgian fronts and also co-founded the successful publishing company Holt, Rinehart, and Winston.

The cliché that "the butler did it" dates from a 1930 mystery novel by Mary Roberts Rinehart called *The Door*, in which a series of strange murders takes place among a wealthy family and its servants. Not to spoil Ms. Rinehart's gifted and spooky plotting for you, but in this mystery—you guessed it—the butler did it!

You're an Ugly American! But Don't Be Offended

The original meaning of the term *ugly American* was quite different from its usage today. In present usage, the term is used to characterize the personalities and behaviors of loud, brash, obnoxious Americans when traveling overseas, who show little concern or appreciation for the foreign cultures they happen to be visiting. Instead, they are oafish, insolent, and stereotypically "ugly" in the way they behave in foreign countries.

Ironically, this couldn't be farther from the original, positive use of the term as expressed in the 1958 novel *The Ugly American* by William Lederer and Eugene Burdick. In this novel, the title term is used in reference to those Americans who travel and work overseas and who do good works helping the local populations. They are "ugly" in the sense that they are mostly anonymous and not seeking of publicity or fame for their achievements, as opposed to other "pretty" types of people whose actions are more flamboyant or designed for publicity and the spotlight. In a most ironic turn, the term *ugly American* has changed from its original, overwhelmingly positive meaning to one of universal derision. Now that's ugly!

PART X
Cool and Unusual People and Places

The Secrets of Isaac Newton, the Magician of Science

The mathematician and philosopher Isaac Newton (1642–1727) is considered by many to have been the greatest scientist who ever lived. But this man—who discovered gravity, invented calculus, and figured out that light is made up of a multi-colored spectrum—also had a number of secrets.

At his death, he left behind over a million unpublished words on magic, the supernatural, and the occult. He never published them during his lifetime for fear of being branded superstitious or behind the times.

Apparently, Sir Isaac Newton had more on his mind than just science.

A highly contentious and argumentative man who often feuded bitterly with other scientists, he also had only two close personal relationships in his life, both with young men. When the second moved out on Isaac, he had a nervous breakdown from which he never fully recovered.

Who would have thought that Mr. Science had such a big closet?

A Cut Above:
What Would You Do to Get a Job?

The word *eunuch*, referring to a castrated male, comes from Greek words meaning "bed keeper," the usual occupation of such eunuchs being to watch over a king's or sultan's harem. The belief was of course that they were safe to leave with the women. As most of these eunuchs were slaves, it's reasonable to assume the castrations were not voluntary. Such was not the case in other parts of the world, especially in China.

There, for more than a thousand years, voluntary castration was a means of gaining employment in the emperor's service. The idea was not to curb the male interest in a harem's females, but if a man could not

> For centuries, eunuchs were powerful politicians in China.

have children, he would have no interest in seizing power to start his own dynasty. For centuries, eunuchs were powerful politicians in China, at times reaching positions of power equal to prime ministers.

The use of eunuchs peaked around 1600, toward the end of the Ming dynasty, with more than 70,000 of them in the Imperial Service at that time. By the fall of the Chinese emperors in 1912, there were but a few hundred left, and there the practice ended.

These powerful, dedicated servants of the Chinese emperors were truly a cut above; it took real cajones to get those jobs!

Pope-Pourri: 2,000 Years of Papal Mindblowers

Their are approximately 900 million Catholics worldwide who all, at least theoretically, owe their allegiance to that one man, the pope who lives in the Vatican. What follows are some interesting facts about just a few of the 265 men who have reigned from the chair of St. Peter and about the tiny city-state of Vatican City in which they have lived.

- Pope John XXIII (1958–63) had a bowling alley installed in the Vatican and used it often.

- Pope John XXIII was also a cigarette smoker and often smoked a pack a day.

- Pope John Paul II (1978–2005) had a cocktail named after him that's made with three parts Polish vodka.

- Pope John Paul II was also an ardent soccer fan; in fact, he reportedly changed the scheduled time of his official installation as supreme pontiff in 1978 so that he wouldn't miss an important soccer game.

- In 1960 Karol Wojtyla, the man who became Pope John Paul II, published a play called *The Jeweler's Shop*. So far as anyone can tell, he's the only pope ever to write a play. In 1988 it was made into a film starring Burt Lancaster.

- In 897 the body of the very dead Pope Formosus (891–896) was dug up nine months after his death and put on trial for illegally usurping the papal throne. Found guilty, he was thrown in the Tiber River.

- Eggs Benedict is named after Pope Benedict XIII (1724–30), who enjoyed the dish for breakfast during the years of his reign.

- The only Pope to ever write a cookbook was Pius V (1566–72), who titled it appropriately enough *The Cooking Secrets of Pope Pius V*.

- Pope Pius XII (1939–58) had a pet canary named Gretchen that he used to let fly around his room. Today the only official pets in Vatican City are five dogs.

- Pope Celestine V (1294) lived in a cave as a hermit directly before he was pope. Less than a year into his reign, he went back to his cave and lived out the rest of his life in it!

- Pope Pius IX (1846–78) had a billiards table installed in the Vatican. Not only did this pool-playing pontiff enjoy the game, he was apparently quite the shark and often played and beat members of his personal guard and entourage with adept skill. It must have been good for him; Pius IX was also the longest-serving pope ever, serving for 32 years.

- The shortest-reigning pope on record was Stephen II, who reigned for a mere four days after his election in 752.

- The current Pope, Benedict XVI (2005–), has given his permission for his blessing to be used on bottles of beer from the Stuttgarter Hofbrau brewing company in his native Germany. Apparently, the Pope is a big fan of the company's product and doesn't mind it being called the "pope's beer." After he became pope, the brewery promptly sent about 200 gallons of the beer to the Vatican.

IN HONOREM PRINCIPIS APOST PAVLVS V BVRG

Which way to the bowling alley, your holiness?

- There are no nationality restrictions on who can be Pope, but those elected so far have been Italians, Frenchmen, Spaniards, Greeks, Syrians, one Englishman, one Portuguese, one Pole, and one German.

ROMANVS PONT MAX AN MDC XII PONT VII

- The Apostolic Palace, the main building in Vatican City and the location of the pope's living quarters, has 1,400 rooms, 1,000 staircases, and 12,523 windows. Many of the buildings within the Vatican were constructed with stone blocks stolen from the Coliseum, Rome's famous arena.

- With no regular schedule, and as undoubtedly the shortest of its kind in the world, the Vatican Railroad runs all of 2,600 ft. through Vatican City.

- The Vatican has approximately 1,000 residents, of which only about 400 are actually citizens of the city-state itself. Vatican citizens do not pay Italian income tax and also do not pay rent or utility bills. Cardinals of the church are automatically citizens of Vatican City, no matter where they live.

- There has not been a fire recorded in Vatican City in over a century. A 20-man Vatican fire department is ready, though, just in case.

- The only two types of direct official business activity carried out in the Vatican are the making of mosaics and the issuing of postage stamps.

- Airplanes are not permitted to fly over Vatican City.

- The name Vatican comes from the Latin word *vates*, meaning "fortune-tellers." In ancient Roman times the current site of the Vatican was a hillside popular with psychics, soothsayers, and fortune-tellers, from which they would do business with the passing public.

- Begun in 1557 by order of Pope Paul IV, the Vatican's *Index of Forbidden Books* included more than 4,000 entries, including *The Count of Monte Cristo* by Alexander Dumas and *The Decline and Fall of the Roman Empire* by Edward Gibbon. It was finally abolished in 1966 by Pope Paul VI.

- The very first person a newly elected pope has to deal with after his election is the papal tailor. Once he's pope, he can no longer wear the garments of a mere cardinal. In anticipation of this event, the papal tailor prepares three or four different-sized pope suits, so that whoever is elected can be roughly fitted into his garments in order to immediately face the world and give his first *Urbi et Orbi* ("To the City and the World") papal blessing from the Vatican balcony. When the rather large-girthed Cardinal Roncalli was elected as Pope John XXIII in 1958, even the largest of pope suit selections was rather small for him. As he and the papal tailor gamely endeavored to get him into the largest of the outfits so he could make his speech, Pope John XXIII joked that everyone wanted him to be pope, except the tailors!

The Angel of Rome:
He Could Hit the High Notes

Alessandro Moreschi (1858–1922) was the last known castrato, a musical category like alto or soprano, but for castrated men who as a result could sing like women. The technique had been used for centuries to create these musical freaks of nature, but it was dying out by the end of the 19th century.

Alessandro sang in the Sistine Chapel choir as a favorite soloist of the popes. Nicknamed "Angelo di Roma," the Angel of Rome, he could definitely hit the high notes, but what a price to pay to be able to do it!

Don't Tell Minnie or Mickey

According to unofficial but reliable sources, the one and only thing Walt Disney was afraid of in his life was mice. Somebody must have slipped him a Mickey.

Seen One Wife, Seen 'Em All

Jigme Singye Wangchuk, the king of Bhutan, a small Himalayan kingdom wedged between India and China, has four wives. Interesting enough on its own, but in following with a long-standing Bhutanese tradition, they are all sisters and dress and prepare themselves to look exactly alike! Together they wait on the king hand and foot and fulfill his every need.

One good thing about it, I guess: four wives, but only one mother-in-law!

Mighty Mini Monaco

Originally the site of ancient Phoenician and Greek temples honoring Hercules, and founded in 1215 as a colony of Genoa, the 0.75 square mile independent principality of Monaco bordering southern France is the second-smallest country in the world after Vatican City.

Monaco is so small that its national orchestra is larger than its army!

Guy Lombardo, Superstar

When most people think of the orchestra leader Guy Lombardo (if they're old enough to remember him at all), it's as the venerable and seemingly eternal New Year's Eve big-band leader who for decades led us all in singing "Auld Lang Syne" as the clock struck midnight.

What most people don't know is that the song was Guy Lombardo's theme song, and it was as a result of playing it for 50 years that it became a hit and a standard on New Year's Eve across America and across the world. Even after the 1970s, when Guy retired and his presence on TV on New Year's Eve was replaced by the likes of Dick Clark and others, Guy's theme song

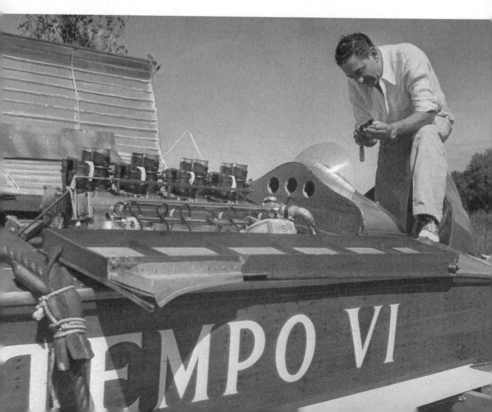

is still the ultimate musical symbol of that night every year for millions, if not billions.

Other things about Guy that most people may not know are that he was born in Ontario, Canada, in 1902; that he had more than 500 hit songs during his career (including "Ain't She Sweet," "Return to Me," and "Footloose and Fancy Free"); that he sold more than 300 million records in his career (far and away the most for any big-band-era act); that his brother and fellow orchestra member Carmen wrote many of Guy's hits; and that in the late 1940s, Guy Lombardo was the American speedboat racing champion for four years in a row.

> My kind of guy: A speedboat-racing champion by day, and a world-famous orchestra leader by night—Guy Lombardo was a modern-day hero.

Guy Lombardo, truly an amazing talent. Next New Year's Eve as you're downing a glass of champagne and crooning "Auld Lang Syne," remember Guy and his big-band orchestra that surely played "the sweetest music this side of heaven."

Academia Nuts:
So You're the Expert, Eh?

From time to time, even the brightest and most well-respected of us are prone to the most bewildering opinions and statements imaginable. The following are presented as a prime display of this fact.

"The brain is an organ of minor importance."
—ARISTOTLE, GREEK PHILOSOPHER, 4TH CENTURY BC

"I do not consider Hitler to be as bad as depicted. He is showing an ability that is amazing, and he seems to be gaining his victories without much bloodshed."
—MOHANDAS K. GANDHI, INDIAN LEADER, 1940

"The army is the Indian's best friend."
—GENERAL GEORGE ARMSTRONG CUSTER, U.S. MILITARY LEADER, 1870

(Apparently they didn't believe him; Custer was killed fighting Native American forces at the Battle of the Little Big Horn in 1876.)

"MARTIANS BUILD TWO IMMENSE CANALS IN TWO YEARS—Vast Engineering Works Accomplished in an Incredibly Short Time by Our Planetary Neighbors"
—*THE NEW YORK TIMES* HEADLINE, AUGUST 27, 1911

"By 1940 the relativity theory will be considered a joke."
—GEORGE FRANCIS GILETTE, U.S. ENGINEER AND WRITER, 1929

"Thou knowest no man can split the atom."
—JOHN DALTON, BRITISH PHYSICIST WHOSE EXPERIMENTS LAID THE FOUNDATIONS FOR MODERN ATOMIC THEORY, 1803

"A diamond, which is the hardest of stones, not yielding unto steel, emery, or any other thing, is yet made soft by the blood of a goat."
—SIR THOMAS BROWNE, BRITISH PHYSICIAN AND AUTHOR, 17TH CENTURY

"We need not hesitate to admit that the Sun is richly stored with inhabitants."
—SIR WILLIAM HERSCHEL, ROYAL ENGLISH ASTRONOMER
AND DISCOVERER OF URANUS, 1781

(We can only assume they're well-tanned ones!)

"Louis Pasteur's theory of germs is a ridiculous fiction."
—PIERRE POCHET, FRENCH PROFESSOR OF PHYSIOLOGY, 1872

"Phrenology will prove to be the true science of the mind. Its practical uses...will give it one of the highest places in the hierarchy of the sciences."
—ALFRED RUSSEL WALLACE, BRITISH BIOLOGIST
AND EARLY PROPONENT OF THE THEORY OF EVOLUTION, 1899

(For those who don't know, phrenology is the "science"
of feeling the bumps on the head
to determine personality and psychology.)

"We don't like their sound, and guitar music is on the way out."
—DECCA RECORDS, REJECTING THE SIGNING OF THE BEATLES, 1962

"The telephone has many shortcomings and is inherently of no value to us."
—WESTERN UNION INTERNAL MEMO EVALUATING THE POTENTIAL
OF THE TELEPHONE, 1876

"Who the hell wants to hear actors talk?"
—HARRY M. WARNER, PRESIDENT OF WARNER BROS. STUDIOS, 1927

"Stocks have reached what looks like a permanently high plateau."
—IRVING FISHER, YALE UNIVERSITY ECONOMICS PROFESSOR, OCT. 17, 1929

(Twelve days later the stock market crashed on Black Tuesday, leading to the Great Depression.)

"Everything that can be invented has been invented."
—CHARLES DUELL, HEAD OF THE U.S. PATENT OFFICE, 1899

"Who would want to see a play about an unhappy traveling salesman?"
—CHERYL CRAWFORD, SUCCESSFUL NEW YORK THEATER PRODUCER AND COFOUNDER OF BOTH THE GROUP THEATER AND THE ACTORS STUDIO, REGARDING THE PLAY *DEATH OF A SALESMAN*, 1949

"God himself could not sink this ship."
—A DECKHAND ON THE *TITANIC* SHORTLY BEFORE ITS FATEFUL VOYAGE, 1912

"Forget it, Louis. No Civil War–picture ever made a dime."
—IRVING THALBERG, MGM STUDIOS WUNDERKIND EXECUTIVE TO LOUIS B. MAYER, REGARDING PURCHASING THE MOVIE RIGHTS TO THE BEST-SELLING NOVEL *GONE WITH THE WIND*, 1936

"I believe it is peace in our time."
—NEVILLE CHAMBERLAIN, RETURNING FROM DISCUSSIONS IN MUNICH WITH ADOLF HITLER, 1938

"When the beaver is pursued, knowing this to be on account of the virtue of its testicles for medicinal uses, not being able to flee any farther it stops, and in order to be at peace with its pursuers bites off its testicles with its sharp teeth and leaves them to its enemies."
—LEONARDO DA VINCI, ITALIAN ARTIST AND SCIENTIST, 15TH CENTURY

The gods shall not be mocked. Like so many others in the days leading up to the tragic voyage, a deckhand confidently declared the *Titanic*'s invincibility.

"What are the Bolsheviks? They are representatives of the most democratic government in Europe. Let us recognize the truest democracy in Europe, the truest democracy in the world today."

—WILLIAM RANDOLPH HEARST, U.S. NEWSPAPER PUBLISHER, 1918

"Nobody can overthrow me. I have the support of 700,000 troops, all the workers, and most of the people. I have the power."

—THE SHAH OF IRAN, MOHAMMAD REZA PAHLAVI, 1978

(In January 1979, the shah left the country and the Ayatollah Khomeini assumed control. A little over a year later, the shah was dead.)

The original flyboys: Orville and Wilbur Wright made history at Kitty Hawk in 1903.

"I will ignore all ideas for new works and engines of war, the invention of which has reached its limits and for whose improvements I see no further hope."

—JULIUS FRONTINIUS, CHIEF MILITARY ENGINEER
TO THE ROMAN EMPEROR VESPASIAN, 1ST CENTURY AD

"Man will not fly for 50 years."

—WILBUR WRIGHT TO HIS BROTHER ORVILLE, 1901

*(Two years later at Kitty Hawk, Orville and Wilbur
made history with the world's first successful flight
of a powered aircraft.)*

"We know, on the authority of Moses, that longer ago than 6,000 years the world did not **exist**."

—MARTIN LUTHER, GERMAN PROTESTANT REFORMER, 16TH CENTURY

"Woman may be said to be an inferior man."
—ARISTOTLE, GREEK PHILOSOPHER, 4TH CENTURY BC

"Nature intended women to be our slaves. They are our property. They belong to us just as a tree that bears fruit belongs to a gardener. What a mad idea to demand equality for women! Women are nothing but machines for producing children."
—NAPOLEON BONAPARTE, FRENCH EMPEROR, EARLY 19TH CENTURY

"One half of the children born die before their eighth year. This is Nature's law; why try to contradict it?"
—JEAN-JACQUES ROUSSEAU, FRENCH PHILOSOPHER AND AUTHOR, 1762

"Sensible and responsible women do not want to vote. The relative positions to be assumed by man and woman in the working out of our civilization were assigned long ago by a higher intelligence than ours."
—GROVER CLEVELAND, FORMER PRESIDENT OF THE UNITED STATES, 1905

"No woman in my time will be prime minister."
—MARGARET THATCHER, BRITISH PRIME MINISTER, 1969

(Ten years later in 1979, Mrs. Thatcher became the first female prime minister of Great Britain. She served as prime minister for 11 years, longer than any other British prime minister in the 20th century.)

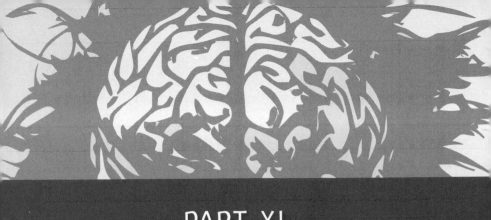

PART XI
Sports and Fatness

Today's Golf Game Has Been Cancelled Due to War

In 1457 in Scotland, the country where golf was invented, the Scottish parliament actually banned the playing of the game for a time. So many young men were playing the game so often it was taking them away from archery practice and threatening the very security of the country.

Incidentally, the meaning of the word *golf* probably comes from its original abbreviation for the words "Gentlemen Only, Ladies Forbidden."

Stay out of the bunker: In 15th-century Scotland, when most young men were more concerned with their short game than the defense of their country, golf was banned.

163

Huddle Up!

The common "huddle" seen on playing fields every weekend during football season had its start at Washington, D.C.'s Gallaudet College for the Deaf. When Gallaudet's all-deaf football team, the Bisons, played, they of course used sign language to communicate.

Legend has it that on a windy fall day in 1894 the Gallaudet football team was losing badly. Quarterback Paul Hubbard some-

Hear ye! Hear ye! Deaf quarterback Paul Hubbard of Gallaudet College is credited with inventing the football huddle.

how suspected that someone on the opposing team knew sign language and was spying on the Gallaudet players and their sign language open-air discussions. Hubbard ingeniously pulled his teammates into a huddle, and the rest is history.

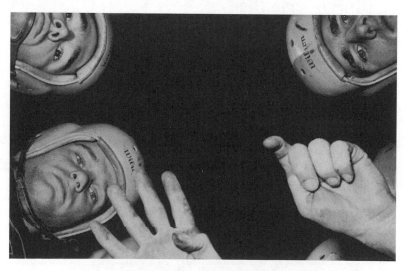

The Hurricane That Spawned a Basketball Star

When NBA super-star Tim Duncan of the San Antonio Spurs was growing up on the island of St. Croix in the U.S. Virgin Islands, he was originally training to be an Olympic swimmer. In 1989 Hurricane Hugo destroyed the island's only Olympic-sized swimming pool. As a result (and to the eternal consternation of NBA coaches across the league), Tim took up basketball! He learned quickly and is today one of the greatest players in the game.

If not for Hurricane Hugo, San Antonio Spurs superstar Tim Duncan might have favored a Speedo instead of his jump shot.

The English Channel Channel: What a Difference a Century Makes

In 1875 the first known swimming of the English Channel, by a man named Matthew Webb, took 21 hours, 45 minutes. In 1994 it took Chad Hundeby seven hours, 17 minutes. I guess he ate his Wheaties.

Yes, but Can He Steal Bases?

The professional major league baseball team today known as the Pittsburgh Pirates was originally known as the Pittsburgh Alleghenies. By "stealing" an unsigned player from another team during the off-season in 1891, the newspapers started calling them the Pirates and the name has stuck ever since.

Why People Are Fat: Preparing for the Famine That Never Comes

People are fat because the human body is doing the job it was taught to do by the last 10 million years of evolutionary schooling. For those 10 million years, as advanced primates heading towards humanness, we were nomadic hunter-gatherers, and every seven years or so there was a famine, a drought, an earthquake, whatever—something that would inevitably interrupt the food chain to us. Therefore, in order to survive, evolution designed us by mutative adaptation to be able to live on next to nothing if need be, and when food was plentiful, to diligently store it away until the next food crisis. Being able to get fat was an important and distinct evolutionary advantage!

With the advent of agriculture only about 10,000 years ago, we began to stay in one place and gradually get a handle on the food thing. And that's why people are fat; because their bodies are doing the job of storing food away, but storing food away for a food crisis that never comes!

Additionally, to get a handle on weight control, one must first grasp this related fundamental understanding about how the body uses fuel.

The body will always burn fat last as fuel; stored fat is the last resort for energy against the famines and food crises of ancient days. Things like refined sugar, alcohol, caffeine, and other things are super fuel for the 10-million-year-old human body, and it will burn them instead of fat any day.

And that, in my humble opinion, is why people are fat.

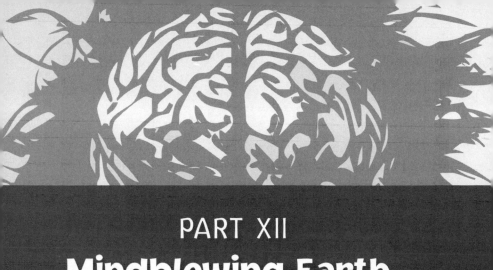

PART XII

Mindblowing Earth, Space, and Time

Water, Water Everywhere, but Only 1 Percent to Drink

Water is the most common substance found on the Earth, and 75 percent of Earth's surface is covered by it. Water is the only substance on the Earth found naturally in all three states of matter: solid, liquid, and gas.

Ninety-seven percent of the Earth's water is found in the oceans, and only about 1 percent of the world's water is drinkable.

Seventy-five percent of this drinkable water is locked up in the world's ice caps at the poles. If all the water in ice packs and glaciers were to melt, the level of the sea would rise over 200 feet. The ice pack known as the Antarctic Ice Sheet alone is almost twice the size of the United States.

We use the same water the dinosaurs used. In a 100-year period, a molecule of water spends roughly 98 years in the ocean, 20 months as ice, about two weeks in lakes or rivers, and less than a week in the atmosphere. Each day the sun evaporates about a trillion tons of water.

Sixty-six percent of the human body is water, bones are 25 percent water, the brain is about 70 percent water, and human blood is 83 percent water.

Seventy-five percent of a chicken is water and 95 percent of a tomato is water.

Humans need about two and a half quarts of water a day to survive. A human can live almost a month without food, but only about a week without water.

The average American uses about 100 gallons of water a day, most of it in the bathroom, kitchen, watering lawns, or washing cars. 500 years ago, the average human used about five gallons a day. People in the U.S. use as much as 700 billion gallons of water every day. There are more than a million miles of water pipes in the U.S., enough to circle the globe more than 40 times!

Two percent of U.S. homes have no running water.

According to NASA, the natural rotation of the Earth has actually been altered slightly by the more than 10 trillion tons of water stored in reservoirs around the world.

Tutunendo, Colombia, is the world's wettest place, averaging over 450 inches of rainfall a year. The world's driest place is the Atacama Desert in Chile, which, until it received a light shower in 1971, had not received a single drop of recorded rain in more than 400 years.

In some parts of the Earth, rain is so uncommon that the natives do not have a word in their vocabulary for it.

Water was the first word spoken by Helen Keller and the last word spoken by President Ulysses Grant. Getting thirsty?

H 2 oh! In a 100-year period, a molecule of water spends roughly 98 years in the ocean, 20 months as ice, about two weeks in lakes or rivers, and less than one week in the atmosphere.

The World Has Gone to Pot, Many Times

The cultivation of the hemp plant (also known by its Spanish name "marijuana") for paper and textiles goes back more than 10,000 years to Asia. Hemp cultivation in Europe began around AD 200.

The first Bibles ever printed were printed on hemp paper.

In the early history of the Americas after Columbus, there were places where the mandatory growing of hemp was enforced by law. Well into the 1700s, American colonists could legally pay their taxes with hemp.

George Washington and Thomas Jefferson both grew hemp.

The first American flag was made out of hemp fabric, and the first drafts of both the Declaration of Independence and the U.S. Constitution were written on hemp paper.

Ben Franklin used hemp pulp in the country's first paper mill, and the oil used in Abe Lincoln's lamp to read at night when he was growing up was extracted from the hemp plant.

Before the late-19th century, virtually all the ships that sailed the seas used rope and sails made from hemp. The prairie schooners and Conestoga wagons that the pioneers used to settle the American West were covered with hemp canvas. Indeed, the very word *canvas* comes from the Arabic word for hemp. The original Levi's jeans were made from hemp.

In 1937 several different fear-mongering groups erroneously linked hemp to dangerous drug use and had it outlawed by an act of Congress.

In 1941, with the loss of access to sources of hemp, jute, and sisal from Asia following the attack on Pearl Harbor by the

Japanese, the U.S. government launched the "Hemp for Victory" program, and the growing of hemp soared. Under slogans like "Grow hemp for the war," thousands of acres were planted. Among the vital uses of this homegrown hemp were twine and rope for the navy and others, light-duty fire hose, shoelaces for soldiers' boots, and parachute webbing for U.S. paratroopers and airmen.

Following the end of World War II, hemp was again made illegal by an act of Congress in 1955.

An acre of hemp produces four times the paper as does a comparable acre of trees and can grow back in less than a year.

George Washington and Thomas Jefferson both grew hemp.

Hemp is a more prolific producer of ethanol fuel than corn.

Hemp is one of the strongest natural fibers known, over three times as strong as cotton.

In 1988 a U.S. district court ruled that hemp is "safer than most of the foods we eat."

As a medicine, hemp is a virtual miracle drug when clinically used to treat certain types of pain, nausea, muscle spasms, and lack of appetite. It also helps alleviate symptoms of glaucoma, AIDS, multiple sclerosis, migraines, and numerous other ailments.

Every year over 400,000 Americans die from smoking tobacco, whose only other practical use is as an insecticide. There has never once been a single proven death from the smoking of hemp.

Guess which one is illegal.

Meet the Beetles

Of the approximately 2,250,000 animal species living on the planet today, 800,000 are insects! And of these 800,000 insect species, 300,000 are beetles! Nature must like them because there are far and away more varieties of beetles on the Earth than of any other living creature.

There are approximately:

- 4,300 species of mammals (including us)

- 9,000 species of birds

- 27,000 species of fish

- 3,000 species of amphibians

> Of the 800,000 insect species, 300,000 of them are beetles.

- 8,000 species of reptiles

- 800,000 species of insects

The other approximately 1.4 million animal species are bacteria, viruses, fungi, molds, and other assorted little wiggly creatures.

I'll Be Your Host Tonight

You're covered in 'em! Bacteria, viruses, insects, worms...
And inside you, too!

You, human, are infested!

You've got between 500 to 1,000 different species of bacteria living in you and on you right now. Many are beneficial, some are neutral, and some can be deadly. As bacteria are smaller than human cells, you've actually got 10 times as many bacteria in you as you have human cells! Most of the bacteria live in your mouth, your guts, or on your skin.

As for viruses, you may have as many as 15 to 20 of these living in you and on you right now. Everything from little wart viruses to cold and flu viruses to things like West Nile Virus and Ebola! (Hopefully not.) Viruses are so small, much smaller than bacteria, that some viruses actually live and feed on bacteria while the bacteria are living and feeding on you! It's also been estimated that there are up to 1,500 virus DNA "skeletons" in our own DNA that we've conquered and assimilated over the millennia.

If you like bugs (or even if you don't), say hello to your little friends: thousands of dust mites, eyebrow mites, and other tiny skin- and hair-dwelling critters all over you right now! Little arachnids, insects, protozoans, etc., that are mostly non-harmful, just crawling all over you night and day, eating your dead, flaking skin or feeding on you in a myriad of other ways.

And what of the lovely parasitic tapeworm? These little beauties can grow up to 30 feet long in your gut and can lay one million eggs a day inside you! They can eat so much of your ingested nutrients that you can feel hungry despite continuous eating, and you'll still look fat because of severe water retention caused by the tapeworm's presence inside you! Other particularly effective internal worm parasites include pinworms and hookworms.

And we haven't even mentioned other, more visible human-body companions like fleas, ticks, lice, mosquitoes, and flies.

Sleep tight. You're not alone!

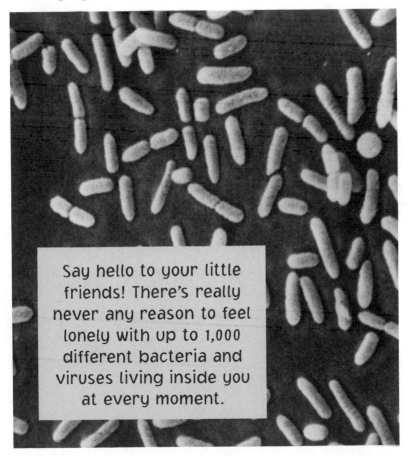

Say hello to your little friends! There's really never any reason to feel lonely with up to 1,000 different bacteria and viruses living inside you at every moment.

Slow Down, Baby! Do You Know How Fast You Were Going?

The next time someone tells you that you are too slow or too much of a couch potato, use the following information to leave them in the dust!

As someone sitting or standing on the surface of the spinning Earth
—You're traveling about 900 mph right now!

As an occupant of the Earth as it journeys around our Sun on its yearly voyage
—You're traveling about 66,000 mph right now!

As a member of our Solar System, orbiting around the spinning Milky Way galaxy
—You're traveling about 500,000 mph right now!

As a member of our Galactic Cluster, hurtling away from the Big Bang that started it all
—You're traveling about 700,000 mph right now!

That should prove to them once and for all that you're not a stick in the mud!

Crowded House

Our galaxy is the Milky Way, and it is made up of about 200 billion stars including our Sun. Until the 20th century, astronomers thought that the Milky Way was the whole universe!

With the advent of more powerful and sophisticated telescopes, we now know that the Milky Way is one of perhaps as many as 200 billion galaxies!

Each of these 200 billion galaxies may have from 100 billion to 1 trillion stars in it.

You do the math. We're talking trillions upon trillions of stars and therefore trillions upon trillions of potentially life-giving planets that could be orbiting them.

It may be a long drive, but we almost assuredly have a lot of neighbors.

There could be as many as two billion galaxies in the universe, each with up to trillions of stars in it.

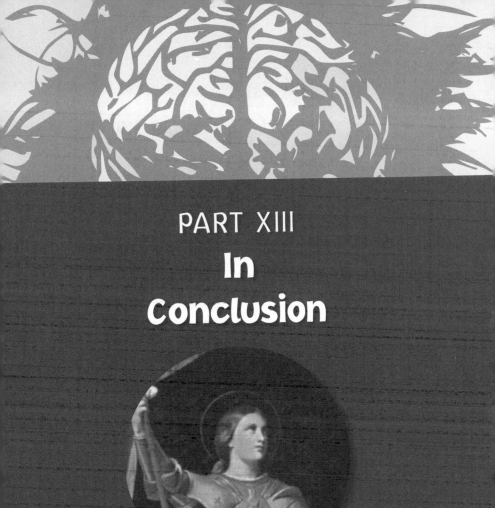

PART XIII
In
Conclusion

Famous Last Words

As we approach the end of this book, it might now be appropriate to take a look at some of the final utterances of certain notables at their hour of passing on to that other great Mindblower, death itself.

- Dylan Thomas (1953)—"I've had 18 straight whiskies. I think that's the record."

- Francisco "Pancho" Villa (1923, *beseeching a journalist as he lay dying*)—"Don't let it end like this. Tell them I said something."

- H.G. Wells (1946)—"Go away...I'm alright." (*He wasn't!*)

- Ludwig van Beethoven (1827)—"I shall hear in heaven."

- Humphrey Bogart (1957)—"I should never have switched from Scotch to Martinis."

- Lou Costello (1959)—"That was the best ice-cream soda I ever tasted."

- General John Sedgwick (1864, *Union Army general killed in battle during the U.S. Civil War*)—"They couldn't hit an elephant at this dist..."

- Joan of Arc (1431)—"Hold the cross high so that I may see it through the flames."

- St. Lawrence (258, *while being burned to death in Rome for his Christian faith*)—"Turn me over. I'm roasted on one side."

- Henry David Thoreau (1864)—"Moose...Indian..."

- Oscar Wilde (1900)—"Either that wallpaper goes or I do."

- Karl Marx (1883)—"Last words are for fools who haven't said enough."

Joan of Arc: she burned for France.

Hey, Abbott! Can I have another soda?

Some Mindblowing Final Thoughts

In this truly dazzling universe and world in which we all live, there is beyond any doubt an endless parade of Mindblowers yet to come, both in the rediscovery of history and in the future ahead of us. For someone like me who delights in the mystery, the irony, and the insight that is gleaned from such events, it is only a matter of time before I will begin working on *Mindblowers II!* Thanks for traveling along on this journey with me. I look forward to seeing you again farther on down the road.

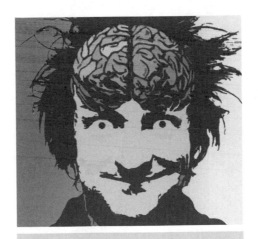

'Tis an ill wind
that blows no minds.

Acknowledgments

I'd like to acknowledge Mitch Rogatz, Tom Bast, Amy Reagan, Linc Wonham, and everyone else at Triumph Books for helping bring *Mindblowers* to the light of day. Additionally, thanks to Paul Levine, my attorney, for his help with contractual negotiations, understandings, and obligations. Special acknowledgments also go to Ron Geiger, Owen Taylor, Lorraine Axeman, John McCoy, David Hoyt, and Matthew Sherman for crucial feedback at critical times in this process. Thanks to one and all.

Selected Bibliography

Abdul-Jabbar, Kareem, and Alan Steinberg. *Black Profiles in Courage*. New York: Harper Collins Publishers, 1996.

American Heritage Dictionary of the English Language. Fourth Edition. Boston: Houghton Mifflin Company, 2000.

Aron, Paul. *Unsolved Mysteries of American History*. New York: John Wiley & Sons, 1997.

Bartlett's Familiar Quotations. Seventeenth Edition. Boston: Little, Brown and Company, 2002.

Beyer, Rick. *The Greatest Stories Never Told*. New York: Harper Collins Publishers, 2003.

Boller, Paul F., Jr. *Not So! Popular Myths about America from Columbus to Clinton*. New York: Oxford University Press, 1995.

Brewer's Dictionary of Phrase & Fable. Fifteenth Edition. New York: Harper Collins Publishers, 1995.

Cerf, Christopher, and Victor S. Navasky. *The Experts Speak*. New York: Pantheon Books, 1984.

Duffy, Eamonn. *Saints & Sinners: A History of the Popes*. New Haven: Yale University Press, 1997.

Encyclopedia Americana. International Edition. Danbury, CT: Grolier, Inc., 1994.

Encyclopedia Britannica. Fifteenth Edition. Chicago: Encyclopedia Britannica, Inc., 2002.

Facts on File Encyclopedia of Word and Phrase Origins. Revised and Expanded Edition. New York: Facts on File, Inc., 1997.

Fair, Charles. *From the Jaws of Victory*. New York: Simon And Schuster, 1971.

Farquhar, Michael. *A Treasury of Royal Scandals*. New York: Penguin Books, 2001.

———— . *A Treasury of Great American Scandals*. New York: Penguin Books, 2003.

Felton, Bruce. *What Were They Thinking? Really Bad Ideas throughout History*. Guilford, CT: The Globe Pequot Press, 2003.

Flexner, Doris. *The Optimist's Guide to History*. New York: Avon Books, 1995.

Flexner, Stuart, and Doris Flexner. *The Pessimist's Guide to History*. New York: Harper Collins Publishers, 2000.

Ford, Sr., Henry. *The International Jew*. York, SC: Liberty Bell Publications, 2004.

Forstchen, William R., and Bill Fawcett, eds. *It Seemed Like a Good Idea...a Compendium of Great Historical Fiascoes*. New York: Harper Collins Publishers, 2000.

Frommer's Scandinavia. Twentieth Edition. New York: Wiley Publishing, Inc., 2003.

Hofmann, Albert. *LSD: My Problem Child*. Los Angeles: J. P. Tarcher, Inc., 1983.

Hornsby, Jr., Alton. *Chronology of African American History*. Detroit: Gale Research, Inc., 1991.

Kick, Russ. *50 Things You're Not Supposed to Know*. New York: The Disinformation Company, 2003.

Knutson, Roger M. *Fearsome Fauna: A Field Guide to the Creatures That Live in You*. New York: W. H. Freeman and Company, 1999.

Lederer, William, and Eugene Burdick. *The Ugly American*. New York: W.W. Norton and Company, 1999.

Lo Bello, Nino. *The Incredible Book of Vatican Facts and Papal Curiosities*. Ligouri, MO: Ligouri Publications, 1998.

Louis, David. *2,201 Fascinating Facts*. New York: Ridge Press, 1979.

Munn, Michael. *John Wayne: The Man behind the Myth*. New York: New American Library, 2004.

Murphy, Edwin. *After the Funeral: The Posthumous Adventures of Famous Corpses*. New York: Citadel Press, 1995.

Murray, Peter, and Linda Murray. *Oxford Companion to Christian Art and Architecture*. New York: Oxford University Press, 1996.

Nash, Jay Robert. *Almanac of World Crime*. New York: Bonanza Books, 1986.

O'Brien, Cormac. *Secret Lives of the U.S. Presidents*. Philadelphia: Quirk Books, 2004.

Olson, Steve. *Mapping Human History*. New York: Houghton Mifflin Books, 2002.

Open Bible. Expanded Edition of the King James Version. New York: Thomas Nelson Publishers, 1985.

Orbanes, Philip. *The Monopoly Companion*. Boston: Bob Adams, Inc., 1988.

Oxford Dictionary and Thesaurus. American Edition. New York: Oxford University Press, 1996.

Petras, Kathryn, and Ross Petras. *Unusually Stupid Americans*. New York: Villard Books, 2003.

Rinehart, Mary Roberts. *The Door*. New York: Kensington Publishing Corp., 1998.

Ridley, Matt. *Genome*. New York: Harper Collins Publishers, 2000.

Robinson, John J. *Dungeon, Fire and Sword*. New York: M. Evans and Company, 1992.

Ross, Shelley. *Fall from Grace*. New York: Ballantine Books, 1988.

Stephens, John Richard. *Weird History 101*. Avon, MA: Adams Media Corporation, 1997.

Tuleja, Tad. *American History in 100 Nutshells*. New York: Ballantine Books, 1992.

Voorhees, Don. *The Book of Totally Useless Information*. New York: Carol Publishing Corporation, 1993.

Warner, Matt. *Cats of the World*. New York: Ridge Press, Inc., 1983.

White, Michael. *Isaac Newton: The Last Sorcerer*. New York: Perseus Books, 1997.

World Book Encyclopedia. 1999 Edition. World Book, Inc., 1999.

Websites

BBC News (news.bbc.co.uk)

Gallaudet University (www.gallaudet.edu)

Information Please Almanac (www.infoplease.com)

Internet Movie Database (www.imdb.com)

Microsoft Encarta Online Encyclopedia
(www.encarta.msn.com)

Nobel Prizes (www.nobel.se)

Smithsonian Magazine (www.smithsonianmag.si.edu)

SPAM (www.spam.com)

Triumph Books (www.triumphbooks.com)

United States Military Academy at West Point
(www.usma.edu)

U.S. National Archives and Records Administration
(www.archives.gov)

White House Pets (www.presidentialpetmuseum.com)